Edward E. Pettee

Block Island

Edward E. Pettee

Block Island

ISBN/EAN: 9783743321816

Manufactured in Europe, USA, Canada, Australia, Japa

Cover: Foto ©ninafisch / pixelio.de

Manufactured and distributed by brebook publishing software (www.brebook.com)

Edward E. Pettee

Block Island

BLOCK ISLAND, R. I.

ILLUSTRATED:

WITH A

DESCRIPTIVE SKETCH

AND

OUTLINE OF HISTORY.

BY EDWARD E. PETTEE, LL. B.

BOSTON:
PRESS OF DELAND & BARTA,
1884.

Preface.

The object of this little volume is to furnish a cheap, comprehensive, and reliable handbook for the use of visitors, or those contemplating a visit to Block Island.

Owing to the loss of the manuscript, just as ready for press, the matter has been entirely rewritten in a hurried manner during the past two weeks, while imperative professional duties were demanding attention.

The writer trusts, however, that his work may still prove acceptable and fulfil the original design.

EDWARD E. PETTEE.

Boston, June 16, 1884.

Formation and Topography.

As the traveller approaches Block Island, the whole situation is one of absorbing interest. The cool sea breezes produce a sense of exhilaration, while the landscape that rises to view is one of singular novelty and beauty.

Surrounded by heaving billows, the island springs up Minerva-like, complete, from the blue waters of the ocean, its rude and lofty bluffs on either hand, spread out between which, and over the long, smooth, crescent beach, are seen receding in graceful undulations, its billowy, emerald surface, its softly rounded hills and valleys, with occasional glimpses of some of the sparkling ponds that nestle in every dale, the great hotels in the foreground, and hundreds of farmers' and fishermen's cottages picturesquely dotting the whole.

At some not very remote period, Block Island undoubtedly formed the eastern extremity of Long Island, having been detached from Montauk, possibly by some convulsion of nature, but more likely by the combined action of wind and sea, which latter force has since, by gradual encroachment, principally on the Montauk side, widened its channel, until at present some thirteen miles of comparatively shoal water intervenes.

As a basis for this presumption we take the fact that the geological structure of the two is peculiar and similar, while entirely unlike that of the adjacent mainland, and the estimate of the New York State Geologist that "at least one thousand tons of Montauk Point is carried away by the sea on a daily average," making an annual degradation of several acres, and finally, Indian traditions indicating that the distance between them was much less in early times.

This theory may seem improbable to many who are unfamiliar with the ceaseless work of these great natural forces in modifying coast contours, but it is certain that much more marvellous changes than this have been wrought by the same agencies at other points within a period covered by authentic records.

The exact position of Block Island is latitude 41° 8' North, longitude 71° 33' West. Its greatest length is about seven miles, and greatest breadth about four miles; in form, pear-shaped, with the small end to the north. The surface is wonderfully diversified, and yet the greatest elevation attained is less than three hundred feet above sea level.

The State Geologist informs us that the surface soil is entirely of granitic origin. No rocks are found in place, and the numerous boulders of granite, of a porphyritic structure, were undoubtedly transported from the mainland by the agency of ice.

FORMATION AND TOPOGRAPHY. 9

LANDING AND STEAMERS.

The substratum on which the whole rests is a deposit of tertiary blue clay, destitute of any remains of marine shells, and containing layers of white sand and imbedded masses of gravelly, bog-iron ore.

On the Crescent Beach are quite extensive deposits of black crystals of magnetic iron ore, known commonly as black sand, which before the invention of blotting paper was extensively used in sand-boxes. At the present time the privilege of its removal is in the hands of New York parties, who have erected a small building in which the sand containing the crystals commingled with the silicious matter is dried by artificial means, then separated by a magnetic engine driven by steam power, after which it is put up in bags and shipped to New York for foundry use.

The soil of Block Island is generally fertile, being, perhaps, better than that of the mainland, and under judicious management, capable of producing large yields of agricultural products.

Although a heavy growth of timber formerly covered the island, of which we have indisputable proof, it had almost entirely disappeared as early as 1750, and was completely stripped during the Revolutionary war, from which time until the present, it has remained wholly destitute of forest trees.

Owing to the scarcity of wood for fuel, this question, at a very early date, was the subject of grave deliberations, as the ancient records bear witness; and had it not been found that nature had amply provided for the exigencies of the case, in the numerous and

HARBOR VILLAGE FROM BEACH.

almost inexhaustible deposits of peat, or "tug," as it is here called, the island must necessarily have been abandoned.

There are three divisions of Block Island commonly recognized by its inhabitants, namely, the East Side, the West Side, and the Neck. The external features, the soil, and the people, of each section differ somewhat. The East Side has been the most favored by nature, and it is in this division that the enterprising inhabitants have concentrated their efforts in the various pursuits of island life. Here the National Harbor is situated, near which is the only considerable village, with its stores, post-office, cable office, life-saving station, hotels, and places of amusement.

The shores of this side have more variety, deeper indentations, boulders grouped in more pleasing manner, and that eminently essential feature of a pleasure resort,—a superb bathing beach, extending in the form of a beautiful crescent, nearly two miles,— a most graceful sweep of pure, clean sand, free from stones and seaweed, and having a gentle descent into the ocean.

This rare and inviting Crescent Beach is one of nature's recent specimens of handiwork. Strange as it may seem, the place it now occupies, less than a hundred years ago, was covered with an almost unbroken line of low hills, or dunes, composed of fine sand, covered with coarse grass, and having a steep slope next the ocean.

FORMATION AND TOPOGRAPHY. 13

CRESCENT BEACH.

The memorable gale of September 23, 1815, caused the first marked change in its aspect, when the tide having risen nearly twenty feet above high-water mark, the sea swept with frightful surges over this portion of the island, denuding the sand-hills and flooding the adjacent meadows, on a portion of which latter it left a deposit of sand several feet in depth. From that time, the hills, divested of their protecting vegetation, were soon levelled by the fierce wintry winds.

From the Harbor, which is described at length elsewhere, the land rises gradually to the south end of the island, where the bluffs are very high and precipitous, rising almost perpendicularly from one hundred to one hundred and seventy-five feet, several portions of which present a singular appearance, having been sculptured into all sorts of grotesque shapes by the furious storms that rally about them during the winter months.

Scattered profusely on the shore, at the base of the bluffs, are huge blocks of granite, both rounded and angular, which serve as barriers to prevent further encroachments of the sea, by breaking the force of the vindictive surges. The loose stones soon become rounded by the continual friction caused by the regular action of the waves. Formerly, large cargoes of these were frequently taken away to furnish pavements for the streets of New York, but the inhabitants soon discovered the ruinous policy of allowing the removal of so important a defence against the inroads of the ocean.

FORMATION AND TOPOGRAPHY. 15

Perhaps the most interesting portion of the bluffs to the tourist is the Mohegan Bluff, so called from the fact that an invading party of Mohegan warriors were driven on to this point, penned up, and barbarously starved to death by the Manisseans.

In his "Recollections of Curious Characters and Pleasant Places," Mr. Charles Lanman says: "These

ROAD TO LIGHTHOUSE.

great bulwarks are both imposing and beautiful, and it is in keeping with the fitness of things that the highest of them should be surmounted by a first-class modern lighthouse, which, though near the brow, cannot be seen from the beach below. Their formation is of clay interspersed with boulders, and hence we find here a greater variety of colors than at Mt. Desert or the Isles of Shoals. The profiles of the

MOHEGAN BLUFFS.

cliffs are both graceful and fantastic, and when looming against a glowing sky, or out of a bank of fog, they are imposing to the last degree; and while you may recline upon a carpet of velvety grass at their summits, you have far below you the everlasting surf of the Atlantic, dashing wildly among the boulders or melting in peace upon the sandy shores.

"But to enjoy this cliff scenery in its perfection you must look upon it under various aspects, — in a wild storm, when all the sounds of the shore are absorbed in the dull roar of the sea coming from afar; in a heavy fog, when the cliffs have a spectral look, and the scream of the gulls is mingled with the dashing of the unseen breakers; at sunset, when a purple glow rests upon the peaceful sea and rolling hills; at twilight, when the great fissures are gloomy, and remind you of the dens of despair; and in the moonlight, when all the objects that you see, and all the sounds that you hear, tend to overwhelm you with amazement and awe."

W. P. Sheffield, Esq., a native of Block Island, portrays the fascinations of this place in an impressive paragraph in his "Historical Sketch," as follows: —

"Those rude gray cliffs, which since their creation, or possibly since the morning stars first sang together for joy, have presented their bared breasts in battle array to the sea and the storm, always had a mysterious attraction to me.

"In my youth no neighboring dwelling or other intrusion came to interrupt the converse of the surrounding scenes with the soul of the solitary visitor. There I saw in the swelling and recession of the mighty bosom of the sea, the respiration of God in nature; there in the calm and lull of the elements, I heard 'the still, small voice' fall upon my ears, moving from above all that was good within me; and in

SOUTHERN CLIFFS.
(From Charles Lanman's Painting.)

the thunder and earthquake shock of the storm, I have often stood almost paralyzed, under the spellbinding influence of the warning voice thus coming from that Power which had aroused the wrath of the forces of nature, and was breaking forth in the war of the elements.

"There I have seen the strong ship, which had traversed every zone, crushed by the power of the ocean

FORMATION AND TOPOGRAPHY.   19

OLD HARBOR POINT.

wave as if her sides were but wisps of straw, and been impressed with the utter powerlessness of man to contend with Him who holds the sea in the hollow of His hand, and with His will directs the storm."

The configuration of the shore between the harbor and Mohegan Bluff is generally pleasing, preserving the outline of greatest resistance to the sea,—a succession of curves. About midway is a little headland called Old Harbor Point, from whence a wild mass of loose rocks juts out into the Atlantic. This Point, and the Pebbly Beach, extending a short distance on its southerly side, and which is made up of myriads of smooth pebbles of every shape and hue, have always been held in high esteem by visitors. If calm elsewhere, the waves break slightly at this point, and in active moods the ocean billows seem more majestic here; but when furious gales whip up the mighty seas that rush on in frightful surges, dashing with stupendous force against the rocks, driving the spray wildly up towards the murky sky, and lashing themselves white with fury, while the huge boulders are hurled about like pebbles in the seething brine, then may one truly feel that he has witnessed a scene supremely grand.

Adjacent to and partially sheltered by the Old Harbor Point was the Old Harbor Landing, once of considerable note, but long since abandoned, and chiefly remembered as the scene of a noted wreck which occurred years ago, and for the visitations of the legendary "Harbor Boys."

LOOKING WEST FROM OCEAN VIEW CUPOLA.

Easterly from the Harbor, and only a few minutes' walk therefrom by a sightly path along the top of the bluffs, which are here from forty to fifty feet above the sea, is a little ravine which the gnawing waves gullied out during a severe storm that occurred some seventy years ago. It extends only a short distance inland, and would be devoid of interest except for the springs which gushed forth thereafter. Their never-failing cool and crystal waters are said to possess valuable medicinal qualities, and are at least ferruginous or chalybeate, as the little, unassuming rills proceeding gently to the sea have stained their pebbly beds a reddish hue. At several points along the eastern shore, similar springs bubble forth, in one instance, more than fifty feet above the sea level. They undoubtedly proceed from island reservoirs and become impregnated from contact with the gravelly bog-iron ore deposits so common.

An eminent living author, writing of the insignificance of the fountains and streams on which the Greeks conferred such imperishable glory, says:—

"Springs seem very trifling things to us,— us barbarians of the North, who only know how to appreciate the colossal. Yet who can ever adequately describe the ineffable beauty of the smallest spring, no matter whether it flows between two flowery banks under the mysterious shade of overhanging trees, or slowly trickles forth from a dark grotto, or jets up in glittering pearls from a pebbly bed, dancing the grains of sand on its tremulous drops."

If we are unable to contemplate a spring without some degree of poetic emotion, how much more vivid must this sentiment have been among our ancestors, who lived in the very bosom of nature!

The shores of the west side are not so diversified as those just described; the bluffs are less picturesque, more gravelly, and have fewer boulders, distributed in less pleasing groups; there is no long stretch of smooth, sandy beach, and the regularity of the outline is wearisome to the eye.

Off the southwest portion lies Black Rock, sunken beneath the surface of the ocean, only discoverable at low tide, and notorious in wrecking annals.

Near this point the bluffs, after having maintained their precipitous character for some four miles along the southern shore, bend around towards the north, and begin to diminish in height and abruptness.

Dickens Point, the most westerly portion of the island, has a very slight elevation, and is of little interest to the tourist. It is diametrically opposite Old Harbor Point, between which two the island attains its greatest breadth, the distance being about four miles.

Between here and Grace's Point, a slight and unimportant projection about two miles further north, are Coonimus and Dorries Coves, formerly of considerable importance, but at present only utilized by a few fishermen as a convenient place to draw their boats above the tide, and where they have built a few small fish-houses. Considerable interest, however,

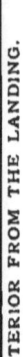

INTERIOR FROM THE LANDING.

attaches to Coonimus, as the seat of one of the Island Wrecking Companies and the location of one of the recently established United States Life Saving Stations.

The view from the bluffs on the southwest portion excels in some respects, for, in addition to the ocean view, with the countless sails dotting the sea and the Sound, Montauk Light, Long Island, and the Rhode Island coast are visible.

They afford charming sites for summer residences, and the foremost to display an appreciation of the attractiveness of this portion of the island is Mr. Thomas E. Tripler, of New York City, who has just completed the erection of an elaborate cottage, which for architectural beauty and completeness of appointments, surpasses any structure on the island.

This portion of the island is traversed by fairly good roads, a drive over which will be found very interesting, and bring to notice many minor features which it is impracticable to recount in detail.

The northerly portion of the island is naturally separated from the main part by the Great Salt Pond, and is now commonly designated as the Neck, though for many years after the first settlers came, it was known as the Corn Neck, from the large quantity of corn yielded by its productive soil, which was found under cultivation at the time of the conquest of Manisses by Massachusetts.

The extreme northern portion terminates in a sharp tongue of land known as Sandy Point, which projects as a bar several miles from the island, and is the dread of mariners, "for here the swift currents that sweep both shores meet, and struggle for supremacy, the bar in terrible combat being alternately laid bare, and swept by seas towering fifty feet above its surface."

This submerged point was formerly an elevated peninsula called the Hummock, on which trees and shrubs grew, and a portion of which existed within the memory of the oldest inhabitants, who speak of it as being only accessible at low tide.

Sandy Point is now occupied by a substantial stone lighthouse, the successor of three others which had been rendered unstable by the shifting sands during a period of thirty-eight years.

The western portion of the Neck embraces the largest area of sandy region on the island, and its shores are the least interesting and most inaccessible of any point.

The beach is narrow, stony, and scarcely relieved its entire length by a boulder or change in form, and is bordered by low sand-hills and shifting dunes.

The eastern portion presents an entirely different aspect,—high, fertile lands divided into well-cultivated farms, broken coast line, with shores of various character, smooth, sandy beaches alternating with stretches of boulders distributed in wild disorder, steep, sloping bluffs deeply serrated and from the summit of which may be obtained one of the most charming views the island affords. The prospect from the promontory, known as Clay Head, so conspicuous to all approaching the harbor, embraces, in addition to the open sea and sheltered Sound, with their hundreds of flitting sails, and the neighboring Rhode Island coast sharply defined on the north, the harbor and village on the opposite side of the beautiful bay, with the hotels, stores, and dwellings, while spread out across the entire breadth of the island, in a grand panorama, are the cottages and farms.

The internal features of the island are peculiar, one of the most striking of which is the profusion of ponds.

Its authorized historian, Rev. S. T. Livermore, says:—"The exact number of these which do not become dry once in ten years has not been ascertained, but they may be estimated at over one hundred without exaggeration. . . . They vary in size from the duck pool to the Great Pond, which is said to cover one thousand acres. The smaller ones are so interspersed as to furnish every farmer with the benefits of from one to twenty ; and as springs are not abundant, and only one stream can approach to the dignity accorded to a small brook, these ponds are of very great convenience for watering animals."

A frequent question asked by the tourist, who marvels at this abundant supply of fresh water is, Whence does it come? There are good reasons for assuming that not a single one of these ponds is sustained by springs, not that it is impossible, but simply highly improbable, from the geological structure of the island, that any springs issue forth from the bowels of the

BLOCK ISLAND BAY.

earth at this point. Possibly a careful examination of the bottom in the depths of the Great Pond might reveal such, but it is unlikely ; and this great body of brackish water, which is comparatively an inland sea, is evidently supplied by the ocean, the narrow strip of sandy soil that confines it on either side operating exactly upon the principle of the well-known Boullay filter. Other ponds in this section of the island are undoubtedly sustained in a similar manner. The formation of those ponds in the elevated hollows and deep little pockets, surrounded by steep hillocks, furnishes the solution of their origin and continuance. They all "have clay bottoms that hold water like caldrons," and are supplied by the rain-fall of the island, which is laid up in its strata precisely as in the hills of the mainland, the small size of the reservoirs being made up for by the frequent rains during a large part of the year, and in summer, protected from exhaustive evaporation by the humid atmosphere which envelopes the island.

The Great Pond, covering a thousand acres, is situated almost exactly in the geographical centre of the island, and nearly divides it from east to west. The strip of land separating it from the sea on the east side is known as the Indian Head Neck, from the circumstance of two Indian heads having been exposed on high poles set in the ancient Indian burial-grounds located on the little bluff that faces the pond.

The narrow rim of land forming its western shore derives its name of Harbor Neck from the location

WINDMILL SCENE.

of the old harbor just inside an inlet called the Breach, that formerly gave communication with Block Island Sound, as the water north and west of the island is designated by the United States Coast Survey.

While the Breach was open, "the fishermen rejoiced in rich harvests of clams, oysters, and other shell-fish," but it was closed many years ago by a violent storm, after which the water became too fresh for their habitation, and is now only tenanted by immense shoals of fish, affording excellent sport for those who are unable to withstand the effect of open sea-fishing.

Near Sandy Point, and covering an area of about an hundred acres, is Saukum or Chagum Pond, also known as Sachem's Pond, from an Indian who stole a canoe here, and attempted to make his escape from bondage. It is very shoal, and its fresh water is supplied by filtration from the sea.

The so-called Middle Pond, lying between the latter and the Great Pond, is fed in the same manner, and is called to mind as the place where the English vessels, during the War of 1812, obtained water, and washed their clothing.

Near the south end of Crescent Beach, and separated from the ocean by a strip of land but a few rods wide, is the Harbor Pond, so called from the fact that, previous to the great gale of 1815, it communicated with the sea by an inlet called the Creek, and which was of sufficient size and depth to allow small sloops to pass inside. At its outlet was situated the

Old Pier, portions of the piling being still visible at low tide.

Immediately north of Harbor Pond is Trimm's Pond, in which is situated a small island called Fort Island, which was formerly occupied by an Indian fortification, and where many bloody battles were fought by the Manisseans with the Mohegans and Pequots, and the scene of a notable encounter between the natives and early settlers.

About a mile south of the centre, on elevated land, lies Fresh Pond or Bass Pond, as more commonly called at the present day. It is perhaps the most important sheet of pure, fresh water on the island. It covers some thirty acres, is "attractive, clear, and surrounded with green shores, in view of pleasant residences," and is resorted to by visitors for black bass and perch, some very fine specimens of which are annually caught. It is of easy access, and reached by way of the Centre, taking the road directly south.

Southeast from the Bass Pond near the road leading from the harbor to the South Light, and about one hundred and fifteen feet above the sea, is Sand's Pond. This extraordinary sheet of pure, fresh water, several acres in extent, is but few feet in depth and located on some of the highest land on the island, yet it never diminishes much in volume, and would afford an abundant supply of the purest of water to the harbor settlement. A movement in that direction was started last year, and a preliminary survey made for the location of an aqueduct, about a mile and a half in length, when it was found that sufficient head would be obtained to force the water to the upper floors of every building about the landing ; but the project was abandoned, owing to the refusal of the parties controlling the pond to dispose of it.

Half-way from the Harbor to the Centre, on the main road, is the old Mill Pond,— a dirty little affair, deserving mention, however, as the site of the mill

THE OLD MILL.

where corn was first ground and wool carded on the island, and also where the first death among the settlers is supposed to have occurred by the drowning of a little child. Remnants of an old mill are still standing, but at the present day the only means of grinding corn on the island is by the two picturesque windmills.

West from the Landing, close by the main road that leads away from the harbor settlement, winding into the interior over the wavelike hills past the smaller hotels and quaint farm cottages, and a mile beyond the little cluster of buildings, consisting of the church, town-hall, two or three stores, and half a dozen dwellings, whose inhabitants assume a certain dignity from the distinction which the name of Centre imparts, rises Beacon Hill, the most elevated point on Block Island. It takes its name from a provision made by the early settlers for their protection, by a blaze from this point warning the inhabitants of the approach of enemies.

From its summit, nearly three hundred feet above the sea, one may obtain a magnificent prospect for miles on all sides. The culminating point is occupied by a little tower, affording shelter and the use of a good glass for a nominal sum. "The landscape, viewed from this eyry, is exceedingly novel and pleasing, comparable with no bit of scenery along the coast." Spread out beneath and encircled by a zone of glistening surf, lies the entire island, with its graceful contour delicately traced on the face of the great deep, "every suggestion of barrenness hidden by green pastures and smiling meadows," variegated by deeper colored patches under cultivation, and checked off into all sorts of odd designs by the several hundred miles of time-stained boulder walls. Sprinkled about in the most irregular manner are the farmhouses, "each surrounded with its cluster of out-buildings, and communicating with the highway by a grassy lane, which often winds through the fields for a mile before reaching its destination."

The softly turned hills, of every conceivable shape, sink gradually away to the sea, like some rich drapery, in every fold of which there "glimmers a pond, fed from some hidden source, and covered with fronds of pond-lilies fragrant in their season with great creamy white blossoms."

Looking out over the azure waters, we see on the north the whole Rhode Island coast line, and in clear weather some of the headlands of Massachusetts and Connecticut ; while on the west are Long Island and others at the entrance to the Sound, belonging to New York, thus bringing to view from this little eminence portions of four States ; and after sunset

> "From the dim headlands many a lighthouse gleams.—
> The street-lamps of the ocean."

Whether looking down the dim, long vista of the Sound, or seaward over the all-embracing waters which separate, yet join, all countries and islands, we see hundreds of seeming chips of boats, with their white wings, traversing this generous "park of pleasure" and pathway for every people.

HARBOR.

There is no natural harbor at Block Island, and the vital question of providing a suitable landing-place and an anchorage for their boats was among the earliest that engaged the attention of the first settlers. Nothing satisfactory was accomplished for nearly twenty years, when in 1680, a harbor company having been organized, a channel was cut through the narrow rim of sand on the west side of the Great Pond, connecting it with the sea. This inlet soon became so navigable "that vessels of seventy and eighty tons burthen actually sailed in the pond." Not proving a profitable enterprise, the company surrendered its charter after fourteen years, when the town undertook to maintain it; but in 1705 it was abandoned altogether, the reason assigned being that "by the providence of God a prodigious storm hath broken down the above said harbor and laid it waste"

After this the inhabitants directed their efforts to the east side, at a point a quarter of a mile north of the government breakwater. Here, previous to 1815, a tide creek, about a dozen feet wide, and of sufficient depth to allow small sloops to pass through during high tide, connected the Harbor Pond with the ocean.

LOOKING ACROSS THE NECK.

About 1705, work was commenced at the outlet of the creek, and what seems to have been a very convenient landing-place completed soon after, which was called the Pier.

LANDING AND BOATS.

After being repeatedly damaged by storms, and abandoned for years at a time, during which intervals various lottery and other schemes for raising funds to repair or build another were unsuccessful, it was finally totally demolished during the great gale of 1815, at which time the creek was choked up by the sand and wash carried over the low lands by the enormous tidal wave. At low tide may still be seen remnants of the piling, against the sides of which planks were placed, backed up with boulders and small stones, and forming a sheltering point.

Soon after this disastrous gale, the inhabitants began the construction of a novel landing-place on the beach near the present harbor. "This was an individual enterprise, each man, as he chose, at low tide, setting his own spiles, where they are now seen," and having been continued for years by a large number of people, it soon became, and continued for over fifty years, the principal harbor, the poles at one time having been more than a thousand in number.

This primitive mode of landing was entirely inadequate to the demands of the island, and at length some of the more progressive among the islanders began to agitate anew the question of a government harbor, which, as early as 1838, had been favorably considered by Congress, but no further action taken. After a lapse of over thirty years, and a determined struggle over the matter, Congress finally made a small appropriation in 1870, mainly through the efforts of Hon. Nicholas Ball, who secured petitions from the Chambers of Commerce in New York, Boston, Philadelphia, and other cities, and represented the cause before the Senate Committee, as a citizen of Block Island.

Work was commenced in October, 1870, and completed in November, 1878. Congress, in the mean time, making the appropriations necessary to carry

40 *BLOCK ISLAND.*

GOVERNMENT BREAKWATER.

on the work, the total cost of which was $155,000,— less than half the sum estimated by the government engineers. The main wall extends one thousand feet into the sea, at which point there is eighteen feet of water at low tide. Two hundred feet further out is a detached section, three hundred feet long, curving slightly inward, at the end of which, fifteen hundred feet from the shore, there is twenty-four feet of water. The original plan was to place still another detached section, of three hundred feet in length, a few hundred feet further north, and at nearly right angles with the main structure, affording shelter from the north winds ; but Congress failed to provide the necessary means. The breakwater is built of heavy blocks of granite, brought from the mainland, and heaped carelessly in the peculiar form of construction known as rip-rap, and contains about 93,000 tons of stone, forming an admirable protection against the waves of the Atlantic.

Here is the home of the Block Island fleet, and the location of the fish-houses incident thereto, adjacent to which are the stores, life-saving stations, telegraph office, and numerous dwellings, while "perched on the high grounds, back of the harbor, are the numerous hotels, which have sprung up like mushrooms since the larger steamers have made the island a stopping place."

HOTELS.

THE establishing of a National Harbor at Block Island marks the beginning of a new era. Previously to the construction of the breakwater, no decked vessel could land, by reason of which, many were deterred from visiting the island, not caring to subject themselves to the inconvenience and risk of landing in a small boat through the surf, which was often attended with much difficulty, requiring great skill and courage on the part of the boatman.

This picturesque little island, which a few years ago was comparatively unknown, is now, by reason of its natural charms, equable climate, and superior advantages afforded to the health and pleasure seeker, coupled with genuine Yankee enterprise in developing and bringing to public notice its excellent hotel accommodations, justly entitled to rank among the leading coast resorts of the States.

Although a public house was opened as early as 1842 on the site of the present Adrian House, and in 1858, three public houses, with combined accommodations for about one hundred guests, were in operation, they were patronized by a limited few, who chiefly resorted there to enjoy the fishing, for which its waters have always been and still are famous.

As soon as the success of the harbor was assured, large steamers visited the island, carrying hundreds of people, curious to see this hitherto almost inaccessible place, which had become widely known through the vigorous efforts made in its behalf in Congress and elsewhere.

In 1873, Hon. Nicholas Ball, to whose enterprise and persistency in the matter are chiefly due the acquirement of the breakwater, erected the Ocean View Hotel, which from time to time, as the needs of the public have demanded, has been enlarged, until at present it exceeds in size, perhaps, any summer hotel in the New England States. It has a charming location, about five hundred feet from the landing, on a high bluff overlooking the harbor and ocean, surrounded by spacious grounds, and rightly named the Ocean View, as from three sides of the house may be had an unobstructed view of the briny deep, while from the gallery at the east end, which extends to within a few feet of the bluff's edge, one may look down on the brown, moss-covered boulders, which the frowning waters of the Atlantic dash over in fury, or sparkling waves, resplendent with sunlight, caressingly infold in peace.

The Ocean View is a well-equipped and well-conducted house, with good-sized, airy rooms, not elaborate in their fittings, but comfortably furnished, lighted with gas, and communicating with the office by electric bells. The table compares favorably with other prominent hotels on the coast, the service is excellent, and the sanitary arrangements unsurpassed. It is 330 feet long and 170 feet deep, the main structure being three stories high, plain and substantial. About 250 feet west is situated the

MOONLIGHT FROM OCEAN VIEW PIAZZA.

Ocean View Cottage, which is connected with the hotel by a bridge which spans the little valley intervening. The combined length of bridge and piazzas is about 1,500 feet, and afford a delightful promenade.

The first floor of the hotel is almost entirely devoted to public rooms, the arrangement of which has been planned in a most judicious manner. Entering near the middle of the north front, the handsomely furnished office is found at the right, near the door, directly opposite which is the bazaar and post-office, connected with which by an archway is a little studio, presenting in itself a very attractive appearance, aside from the exquisite souvenirs and paintings so modestly exhibited. Opposite the main entrance is the immense dining-hall, having a pleasant outlook on the ocean, and a capacity for five hundred guests. Immediately in the rear are the spacious serving-rooms, kitchen, etc., while joining on the west is the servants' and children's dining-hall.

At the extreme west end of the hotel is situated the Music Hall, especially designed for a place of amusement and very handsomely finished. Here the Schumann Orchestra has its home, giving a concert every week-day at noon, and furnishing music evenings for dancing, when the hall is not in use for other entertainments.

Connected with the Music Hall by a broad corridor extending to the east end of the hotel is the large and pleasant drawing-room, arranged so that those who wish may avoid the gayety and necessary noise at the opposite end. Ranging between the two are numerous small parlors, smoking and reading room, toilet-rooms, cloak-rooms, etc.

OCEAN VIEW HOTEL.

In the rear of the hotel, sufficiently distant to avoid all disagreeable features, are the livery stables, steam laundry, cottages for servants, and other outbuildings.

The Ocean View has been under the management of Dr. O. S. Marden, of Boston, since 1877, to whose rare tact, superior business qualities, and untiring application the Hotel and Island unquestionably owe much. Of his success as manager, nothing attests stronger than the unprecedented growth of business and the character and permanence of the guests.

Next approaching in size to the Ocean View is the Spring House, so called from the springs already described, in the little ravine below the house, and from which it is supplied with water by means of a hydraulic ram. Its location is considered by many the finest of any hotel on the island and certainly is a delightful spot. The house is situated about a quarter of a mile south of the Landing, over eighty feet above the sea, several hundred feet back from the bluffs, and is surrounded by a handsome lawn, from which the land falls away in a steep slope allowing an unobstructed view seaward. The Spring House has been in continuous operation since its first opening in 1852. The present proprietor, Hon. B. B. Mitchell, purchased it in 1870, and soon after remodelled and enlarged it, and has since built quite an extensive annex, which is very pleasantly situated a few steps from the hotel. Both combined have a capacity for some two hundred and fifty guests. Most of the rooms have a very pleasant outlook, are well furnished, and in the newer portions of the house large and airy. The general arrangement of the public rooms, to which purpose an abundance of space has been devoted, is very convenient. The furnishings are generally tasteful, and particularly so in the parlor of the annex. The house has always been well patron-

MUSIC HALL, OCEAN VIEW HOTEL.

ized and prosperous, and is under the immediate direction of the proprietor, with whom order and cleanliness is a strong point, and whose personal attention and genial disposition are remembered with pleasure.

About half way between the Spring House and the Landing, and some five hundred feet from the Ocean View Hotel, is the Manisses, by which soft flowing Indian name Block Island was known previous to the present title, bestowed by the stolid Dutchman, Adrian Blok. This house, formerly known as the United States Hotel, was purchased in 1882 by Dr. O. S. Marden, of Boston, and the following winter thoroughly remodelled, and enlarged to double its former capacity, now having accommodations for about two hundred guests.

THE MANISSES.

It is very thoroughly constructed, and generally pronounced the best furnished house on the island. Though its equipments and provisions for the comfort and convenience of its patrons are excellent, its size neither admits of nor demands some features only to be found or expected at a large house like the Ocean View.

The rooms are for the most part good-sized, airy, and neatly furnished, and have electric bells communicating with the office. The light and pleasant dining-hall is well appointed and has abundant capacity for the full complement of guests. The table is maintained at a high standard, the service good throughout, and the sanitary arrangements all that could be desired. The handsomely furnished parlor is at the end opposite the office, with which it communicates by a very tastefully decorated corridor. The dado is the work of Miss Carrie G. Bartlett, who has her studio at the Ocean View.

The piazza on the north side of the house is particularly pleasant, being overhung by a number of handsome poplars, the only tree that seems to flourish on the island,— and a rarity at that,— beyond which the hillside is terraced and ornamented with beds of flowers and has a little fountain in the centre.

The Manisses is under the direction of Miss C. E. Brown, of Boston, a lady of sterling character, marked business ability, and large and successful experience in catering to the public, who makes it her home in the summer, and a home for its patrons.

Pleasantly situated on elevated ground, close by the main road leading across the island from the Harbor and about three fourths of a mile from the Landing, is the Connecticut House, owned and conducted by Mr. M. M. Day, who formerly resided in Connecticut, hence its name.

It is a good-sized house, having accommodations for eighty or more guests, and though some little

distance from the sea, is not without its advantages. It is a substantial, comfortably furnished, and well-kept, moderate-priced house, with large, pleasant rooms, from which a good outlook may be had, either seaward or inland. That the Connecticut House merits the liberal patronage it has received from those desiring a quiet, inexpensive, and homelike place, the writer is well convinced, after occasional contact with its guests, and an acquaintance with the proprietor for several years past.

Not far from the Connecticut House, and reached by a private way, is the Hotel Neptune, situated on a little eminence, surrounded by green fields, and commanding a pleasant prospect. The main structure was built two years ago, as supplemental to the dwelling of the genial proprietor, Rev. W. A. Durfee, who was formerly in charge of the Baptist Church, and is very favorably known to summer visitors. It is a fairly equipped, medium-priced house, and has comfortable accommodations for some seventy-five or more guests.

About half way between the Connecticut House and the Landing, at the branching of the road to the beach, stands the Woonsocket House, which, with rooms in adjacent building, has accommodations for seventy-five guests, and is kept in a very comfortable and homelike manner by Mr. Almanza Rose.

Situated over one hundred feet above the sea and about a quarter of a mile from the Landing, on the road to the South Light, stands the Highland House, from which the land slopes away on all sides, enabling it to command an extended prospect. It has rooms for about seventy-five guests, and is a comfortable, moderate-priced house, run by the proprietor, Mr. D. Alonzo Mitchell.

A short distance to the eastward from the Highland House, a little lower, but similarly situated, is the Norwich House, kept by Mr. J. E. Rose. It is reached by a private way, entering near the Highland House. It has a capacity for only some twenty guests, but affords a very pleasant outlook and a quiet place for those of limited means.

A little distance north from the Highland House, on the opposite side of the road, is the Bellevue House, the name being indicative of its location. It is kept by Mr. M. D. Mott, who provides in a comfortable manner for about twenty-five guests, and patrons speak of the Bellevue House as a very home-like place.

Half way down the hill to the Landing is the Union House, built last year by Mr. L. A. Ball. This house was scarcely in order last season, so it has no established record; but it is conveniently located near the Landing, yet sufficiently aside from the main street to escape the noise and dust; it has rooms for about seventy-five guests, the terms are moderate, and the proprietor, a man of intelligence, disposed to do his utmost for its patrons.

About three fourths of a mile south of the Landing, on very high ground, commanding an extensive prospect, is the Block Island House, opened last season by Capt. Geo. W. Conley, of the steamer "Danielson." It is a plain, substantial structure, supplemental to his residence, with plenty of space about it, and having rooms for about fifty guests. The Captain secured a good number of patrons last season. The writer's knowledge of the house is very limited, but he can commend the proprietor to all as a man of sterling character.

A little distance to the north of the Centre, quite pleasantly situated on a sightly rise of ground, is the Central Hotel. Its proprietor, Mr. Ray S. Littlefield, has, during the past winter, enlarged it to a capacity of about one hundred guests. A new road having been recently opened directly to the beach, though still some distance away, makes the house much more desirable than formerly.

The Pequot House, on the main road, close by the Landing, and having rooms for about sixty guests, is owned and conducted by Mr. D. B. Dodge. It is a comfortably fitted, medium-priced house, well suited to those who enjoy being in sight of the island travel.

A few rods further down the road is the Narragansett Hotel, similarly situated, and with the adjacent building, having rooms for about the same number as the Pequot House, with which it also tallies in other respects. Mr. Randall, who last season was clerk at the Hotel Neptune, has leased it for this season.

On the little point west from the Landing, built on the bluff's edge some twenty feet above the sea, is

Surf Cottage, the residence of Mr. C. W. Willis, who provides in a liberal manner for a few boarders.

Some half a mile north of this point by the Neck Road, and standing a little distance back of the beach, is the Sea Side House, erected preparatory to the coming season. It is somewhat isolated, but is near-

FLEET DRYING SAILS.

est the bathing houses, and rather pleasantly situated. It is to be a moderate-priced house, with rooms for about seventy-five guests.

Close by the Landing, standing where the first public house was opened on Block Island, is the Adrian House, kept by Mr. Nathan Mott. It has rooms for some thirty guests, and is a cheap and popular place, open throughout the entire year.

Rose Cottage is on the hillside near the Spring House. It is the residence Mrs. Matilda Rose, is well patronized and highly spoken of, and has rooms for about twenty guests.

Besides the houses already enumerated, there are many farmhouses where a few boarders are taken during the summer months, and some of which afford superior accommodations, at a very moderate rate.

In addition to the usual varieties of food, the tables are generally abundantly supplied with fish and lobsters, fresh from the sea.

The Block Island mutton has always been famous, and excels in flavor that found in other sections of this country, no doubt owing to the peculiar climatic conditions and excellent grazing.

Public Buildings.

ASIDE from the hotels, the public buildings of Block Island, as may be surmised, are unpretentious and few in number, yet worthy of a passing notice as in a measure indicative of the status of its inhabitants as compared with other rural communities.

At the Centre may be found that indispensable edifice incident to every place, the Town Hall, which in this instance is of very humble proportions, having been originally built by the town many years ago as a meeting-house, and afterwards appropriated for a Town Hall. For some years past it has also been in use as a school-room by the Island High School, having been fitted up for that purpose by the town.

A few rods from the Town Hall stands the First Baptist Church, erected in 1857, and similar in size and general appearance to the average country church. It has a membership of about five hundred, and is in charge of Rev. Charles A. Braithwaite, who commenced his pastorate in 1883 as successor to Rev. W. A. Durfee.

Although among the first settlers there were several devout families, and a deep religious sentiment pervaded the community, the first invitation to a minister to settle there was extended in 1700. The first meeting-house was erected probably in 1756, and the first church organized in 1772.

Situated on the west side, on elevated land, commanding a charming prospect, is the Free Will Baptist Church, which was erected after great efforts on the part of that society, to replace one similar to that at the Centre, which was demolished in the gale of 1869, just before completion.

The reader is referred to Rev. S. T. Livermore's "History of Block Island" for an extended account of the churches and church organizations.

Throughout the island there seems to be a deep sense of respect for the law of God, the inhabitants generally scrupulously observing the Sabbath day, much to the chagrin of a certain class of graceless visitors, who are disposed to desecrate it by fishing excursions. And indeed, how can he "whose life is passed amid the perils of the deep, where thunders roll, and lightings blaze, and yawning waves devour, where rocks and shoals menace and fires consume, how can he live there and be an irreligious man?"

The schools of Block Island have been pronounced by the School Commissioners "as good as those in any of the country towns in the State." In addition to the Island High School, which was first opened in 1875 at the Town Hall, there are five district schools, in charge of well-drilled teachers, and having a good attendance. The school-houses are very plain buildings, but the newer ones are of good size and well arranged.

The Odd Fellows' Hall at the Harbor Village is a plain, substantial building, having a very pleasant hall in the upper story, which is occupied by Neptune Lodge No. 26, organized in 1872. The Atlantic Lodge of Masons also meet here at present, having vacated the hall over the blacksmith shop, a few rods east and across the road.

There is also a flourishing Lodge of Good Templars on the island.

The lower floor of the Odd Fellows' Building is occupied as a confectionery store and ice-cream saloon.

The Block Island Post Office is situated a little distance west of the Landing in the little store building of Mr. C. W. Willis, who is postmaster. Although the office was much improved last season, and affords ample space for its purposes during the larger part of the year, it is entirely inadequate for the handling with facility of the large mails daily brought in through the summer months, and which are annually increasing in volume. Postmaster Willis is very active and obliging, doing his best to fulfil the duties of his office. He does a thriving business in his little shop, which fairly bristles with a most unique assortment of goods.

A few steps west of the Post Office, in a little wing attached to Mr. J. T. Dodge's general store, is the cable office of the U. S. Signal Service, or Military Telegraph, which is available to the public, or for "commercial business," during a large part of the day. The cable extends from a point near the North

Light to Point Judith, about eleven miles distant, and the wires go overland thence to Narragansett Pier, connecting with the Western Union. The rates for messages are for ten words, twenty-five cents, and one cent for each additional word.

The island is well supplied with stores, several of which, especially Mr. C. C. Ball's near the Landing, and Mr. Lorenzo Littlefield's at the Centre, are handsome modern buildings, filled with a large assortment of general merchandise, and add much to the appearance of the place.

At the Landing, situated in the large new building erected by Mr. C. C. Ball, last year, is a neat and well-ordered drug-store, fitted up by Mr. Frank C. Cundall, of East Greenwich, R. I., who is an experienced pharmacist. In addition to a large stock of drugs and medicines, a good assortment of toilet and fancy articles are kept on hand, which the inability of summer visitors in years past to readily procure has often been a source of much discomfort. This new enterprise, especially in behalf of patrons of the hotels, was duly appreciated by them last season, and a gratifying success given to Mr. Cundall.

A little distance further down the road and on the opposite side, Mr. H. Q. Morton, the popular photographer, of Providence, has recently completed a very tastefully finished building, to be used as a studio and residence during the summer months. He is widely known as a very superior artist, and his handsome studio is well worthy of a visit.

LANDING AND STORES.

Government Buildings.

Block Island has two lighthouses, the oldest of which is called the North Light from its situation on Sandy Point, the northern extremity of the island.

It is a very substantial granite building, and was erected in 1867, as the successor of three others, built in 1829, 1837, and 1857 respectively, all of which had been rendered unserviceable by storms and shifting sands. Here was the location of the

> "One set at the mouth of the Sound to hold
> The coast-light up in its turret old,
> Yellow with moss and sea-fog mould."

It is about five miles distant from the harbor, and is reached by the Neck Road, which, after passing over the low, sandy region between the Great Pond and the sea, leads through the fairest portion of the island.

Mr. Hiram D. Ball, the present keeper of the North Light, was appointed by President Lincoln in 1861.

The New or South Light is situated on the southeastern part of the island, near the edge of the famous Mohegan Bluff, and the lantern stands two hundred and four feet above the sea. This is one of the finest and best equipped lighthouses on the coast. It is a handsome brick structure, erected in 1874 at a cost of $75,000, and was first lighted on February 1, 1875. In addition to the lantern-tower, which is about fifty feet high, it contains apartments for the families of the keepers.

Passing through the hallway into the tower, one enters first the oil-room, where is stored in large tanks from nine hundred to a thousand gallons of refined lard-oil, the quantity annually consumed by the powerful lamp. The ascent from the oil-room to the lantern is made by a spiral staircase of iron. Immediately below the lamp is the keeper's room, where a constant watch is kept during the night to keep the flame at the proper height, replace broken chimneys, and see that nothing interrupts the proper workings of the light, on which depends the safety of many thousand vessels that pass this point annually.

A few steps higher up is the lantern, which is about ten feet high and a dozen feet in diameter, the framework of iron, — in fact, no wood is used about the tower, — and containing a magnificent Fresnel Fixed Light of the first order, which is a marvel of ingenuity in the scientific arrangement of the lenses, which cost about $10,000, and consist of a cylindrical hoop of glass as a refracting lens, above and below which are separate glass prisms of triangular section, placed at proper angles to reflect and refract the light, which would otherwise be uselessly expended in illuminating the clouds, or downward in illuminating the floor of the lantern, so that all the light is made to

SOUTH LIGHTHOUSE.

finally pass out in rays parallel to those of the central lens.

The whole is arranged in the form of a hollow cylinder, narrowing at the top and bottom, twelve feet in height and six feet in diameter, in the centre of which is placed the lamp, which is provided with an ingenious self-feeding apparatus, and has four circular wicks, one within another, the largest being three and one half inches in diameter, and the smallest seven eighths of an inch. The flame is surrounded by a chimney, and kept at a certain height constantly. During the long winter nights the lamp will consume two and a half gallons of oil. Through the day the lenses are covered with linen curtains to prevent the rays of the sun from striking the lamp and unsoldering the brass work.

From the balcony that surrounds the tower may be obtained a magnificent sea view.

Mr. H. W. Clark, the keeper of the light, whose courtesy to the thousands who annually visit here will be gratefully remembered, has been in charge since the first opening of the light, and has two assistants.

In addition to the lighthouse, these men have also to care for and operate the fog signal, which is located about a hundred feet to the eastward of it. During fogs and storms, when the light is of little value, the mariners are warned to avoid this dangerous island by the piercing notes of the siren, as it is called. The apparatus consists of a four-horse-power boiler and a trumpet of cast-iron, seventeen feet long in this instance, which directs towards the sea the sound which is made by the siren placed at its small end.

The sound is produced by the rapid revolutions past each other of two flat discs pierced with a great number of small holes. A jet of steam under high pressure is projected against the discs, which revolve past each other more than a thousand times a minute. As the rows of small holes in the two discs come opposite each other, the steam vehemently rushes through, and makes the singular and piercing noise which the siren gives forth.

To provide against any accident that might disable one siren, two are placed in the building, each having its own boiler and being entirely independent of the other.

The South Light is reached by a very good road from the Harbor, branching off from Main Street at the Skating Rink, and thence by High and Dodge Streets to Sands Pond, where a cart-path, passing eastward through the fields, must be taken. The distance by road is about three miles, while by the footpath along the bluff east of the Landing, and thence by cart-paths and lanes, it is less than a mile and a half.

A few steps west of the Landing, on the edge of the bluffs, stands one of the two United States Life Saving Stations located on Block Island. It is a plain, but neatly finished and rather picturesque building, having a boat-room and mess-room or kitchen on the lower floor, and two sleeping-rooms and a store-room above. In this building the keeper, or captain, and crew live from September 1 to May 1.

The crew of six surfmen are chosen from the fishermen of the island by the captain, and are under his command. "Drawing their first breath within sound of the surf, they pass their childhood viewing the sea in all its moods," and being brought in contact with it frequently from early youth to manhood, they gradually acquire an intimate knowledge of their island coast and its bordering currents, rocks, and shoals, and the peculiar characteristics of its surf.

Capt. J. H. Merryman, in an excellent article on the U. S. Life Saving Service, published in *Scribner's Monthly* for January, 1880, from which the accompanying engravings are taken by kind permission of the Century Company, says: "It is an erroneous notion that the experiences of a sailor qualify him for the surf. The sailor's home is at sea. He is rarely called upon to ply an oar in a small boat, particularly in a high surf, and his vocation gives him little knowledge of the surfman's realm, which is the beach and a portion of the sea extending but little beyond the breakers." The surfman, on the other hand, is not necessarily a sailor.

The crew is instructed in the uses of the apparatus by officers of the Revenue Marine.

The various scientific appliances provided by the Government are kept in constant readiness in the boat-room of the station, and consist of a light and strong surf-boat, provided with air-chambers in both sides and at each end. This boat is mounted on a light vehicle, having four wheels with very broad felloes, so that it can be more easily drawn over the sandy beaches by the crew, horses not being provided.

Standing beside the surf-boat is the mortar-cart, a simple, two-wheeled cart with a box-body, in which are kept in readiness the mortar and appliances used

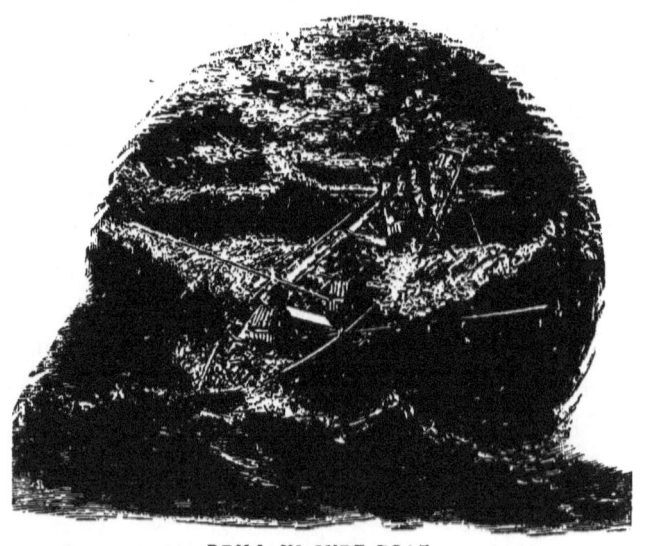

DRILL IN SURF BOAT.
(By permission from the Century Company.)

in rendering aid to shipwrecks. Placed about the room in an orderly manner are the various auxiliary articles sometimes called into requisition.

The mess-room is appropriately furnished and provided with a cook-stove and necessary utensils. The sleeping-rooms contain simply a few narrow iron bedsteads, comfortably fitted up.

The duties of the surfmen during the day are not particularly burdensome, though rather monotonous, and consist chiefly in keeping the building and apparatus in order or preparing their simple meals. At night, however, they become severe, and often fraught with much danger.

The interval from sunset to sunrise is divided into three equal watches, and two of the crew are detailed to patrol the coast during each of these watches, at the beginning of which the men set out in opposite directions, proceeding along the shore, and keeping a sharp lookout over the sea until they meet the patrolmen from the station situated on the west side, with whom certain tokens are exchanged as proof to the captain that this duty has been faithfully performed.

During the severe storms which sweep over the island through the winter months, the path of the patrolman along these exposed shores is often beset with perils. To aid him in tracing his way, he carries a lantern, and is also provided with a signal made of a composition which burns with an intense crimson flame, and which is displayed in case he discovers a vessel too close in for safety, thus warning the unguarded mariners to stand off.

In case a wreck is discovered, the patrolman first burns his signal to apprise the shipwrecked of the fact, then hurries back to report at the station, whereupon the captain, having from the nature of the report decided what course to pursue in the particular case, gives the word of command, and the whole crew are off at once to the scene of the disaster, fully equipped,

When from the nature of the case it is deemed inexpedient to use the surf-boat, the captain orders out the mortar-cart, which is quickly manned. Arriving at the place of the wreck, the well-trained men, each assigned to a particular duty, simultaneously place the various appliances in position, when the mortar is fired, and the shot with line attached is sent flying over the wreck. The shot line is eagerly seized by the unfortunate mariners, who commence hauling it in, the surfmen in the mean time having connected it to an endless line called the "whip," which soon reaches the wreck, bearing a board on which are printed directions, and a tail-block which is soon made fast. The surfmen then commence to operate the whip, to which a hawser or stout rope has already been attached, which is soon on board and firmly secured. The shore end of the hawser, being connected by tackle-blocks to an anchor sunk in the earth, is hauled taut, after which it is raised a dozen feet in the air by means of a wooden crotch which constitutes a sort of pier for this simple suspension bridge. The breeches-buoy, or in some cases the life-car, is slung from the hawser, on which it is drawn to and fro, and the imperilled seamen soon brought safely ashore.

This entire operation has been performed at a practice drill in the incredibly short time of three and one half minutes, and the writer has been present at several such occasions when the actual time consumed was but a trifle more. During actual service, the ap-

GOVERNMENT BUILDINGS. 71

FIRING THE MORTAR.
(By permission of the Century Company.)

paratus of course cannot be put in operation so expeditiously, owing to the stormy weather and lack of skilled practice on the part of the shipwrecked in performing their portion of the work.

The unfortunate sufferers are generally, through exposure and exhaustion, rendered almost helpless, demanding the continued attention of the surfmen, who immediately set about conveying them to the station, where they are provided with dry clothing, warmed and fed, and if necessary, stimulants and such simple restoratives as are kept in the medicine-chest provided by the service, prudently administered, while the wounds of those who may have been injured by the wreckage are carefully dressed. The crew are annually instructed how to perform these remedial duties, as well as drilled in the method for resuscitating the apparently drowned, and procedure in other emergency cases, by an officer of the Marine Hospital Service.

The Life Saving Service was organized in 1871, and is under the management of a general superintendent, who is an officer of the Treasury Department. All its officers are invested with authority of customs officers, thus forming a valuable auxiliary of the Revenue Service. Lack of space prevents the admission of a detailed account of the plan of the organization as well as the result attained, but its efficacy is clearly demonstrated by the reduction of over eighty per cent. in the loss of life by shipwrecks in the various districts, as shown by a comparison of its records with the statistics of the same before the service was established.

LIFE-SAVING CREW AT WORK.
(By permission of the Century Company.)

Wrecking.

The peculiarly exposed situation of Block Island has caused it to be from time immemorial a stumbling block to mariners, and especially to those engaged in the carrying trade along our coast. Its name is prominent in wrecking annals, and conspicuous in the terrible record of marine disasters which have happened all along the ten thousand miles of coast line in the United States.

Even a brief account of the many notable shipwrecks and vessels stranded on its dangerous shores would occupy more space than the limits of this sketch permits.

Twice have six vessels come ashore on the island in a single day, and during one week in the summer of 1880 no less than eleven ran aground here, notwithstanding the Government has guarded its dangerous coast with the best cautionary signals that modern skill has devised to warn the unwary. Although these instances are extraordinary, wrecks have been very frequent, and hundreds of hapless seamen been cast upon its shores during the last two centuries.

The number of lives lost during all these years has been comparatively small, but the loss of property has been enormous, amounting to millions of dollars, while millions more have been saved by the island wreckers.

"The stories and legends of the wreckers so often told and written are calculated to leave very erroneous impressions of the humane exertions of the wrecking bands scattered at intervals along our whole Atlantic coast."

THE BREAKING UP.

The popular ideal wrecker, who is depicted as an ill-omened ghoul, luring vessels ashore by false lights and then swooping down upon them like a bird of prey, may have existed a century ago elsewhere, certainly not here. The modern wrecker is a widely different character, who contributes his skill and individual daring to the unfortunate mariner's aid.

The Block Island wreckers are organized into two "gangs," known respectively as the Old Protection Wrecking Company and the New Wrecking Company. The first named was organized in 1860, and has, between that date and the present time, dislodged and carried into port all sorts of craft, aggregatting in value more than one million and a half dollars. The New Company was not organized until some time afterward, and for a number of years was closely identified with the Old Protection Company, sharing equally in the profits, but in 1876 it became entirely distinct.

Each company is fully equipped with hawsers, lines, cables, anchors, blocks, windlasses, empty casks used in buoying up the stranded vessel, and a variety of large and small boats, all of which is termed "wrecking gear," and stored at convenient stations at various points on the island.

The members are scattered all over the island, and each acts as a watchman for the discovery of wrecks in his vicinity. In case one is detected, the alarm is immediately spread, when all hasten to the place, and if possible a party of them board the grounded vessel and negotiate with the captain for the clearing of his craft, and getting her safely into port. As considerable rivalry exists among the two "gangs," the captain is generally enabled to make a very advantageous contract, which is made in writing, naming the stipulated sum, which is ordinarily about two thousand five hundred dollars, although sometimes not half, and occasionally double, that sum. As soon as the contract is closed, a careful examination is made to ascertain her condition and the best method to pursue in getting her off, which being speedily determined, the necessary gear is at once brought to the scene of action, and operations commenced as early as practicable. Should she have been found to have only touched lightly on the sands, the wreckers set about to lighten and buoy her up by means of empty casks, trusting to flood-tide and the aid of a tug-boat to get her off. When hard aground, these measures are entirely inadequate, so they first sink immense anchors several cables' length abaft of her, from which great hawsers stretch to the wreck, and after being made fast by a perfect network of ropes, so arranged as to distribute the strain as equally as possible to all parts of her, a flood-tide is awaited, when power is applied to the hawsers, which are soon hauled taut by means of a windlass and pulleys connecting with their shore end. The enormous power obtained by the windlass soon hauls the vessel away from the shore toward the anchors, accomplishing what would be impossible to a dozen steam-tugs. Sometimes, however, even this method is unavailing. " In such a case, the wrecker awaits a storm heavy enough to loosen the wreck from the grip of the sand ; it may be days and weeks in coming, but it comes at last, and in the height of its fury the men stand to the windlass, the power is applied, the seas toss her, the tide lifts, the anchors tug seaward with the power of

WRECKERS AT WORK.

a thousand horses. By and by she moves slightly, again and again, and at last, with a supreme effort, she leaves the bar and shoots out to her anchors."

Then comes the often perilous duty of taking her, generally in a badly damaged condition, safely into port, there to receive the thanks of her owners, and obtain their well-earned money.

The wrecker's calling is a very hazardous one, the gangs risking their lives and the considerable capital invested in the various appliances or gear; and although they have in some instances amassed snug little fortunes, they occasionally meet with heavy losses, as they take the entire risk of losing the vessel and their property. Sometimes, when their labors are almost ended, a severe storm will come, and the hawsers chafe and part, when the ship is again dashed among the breakers, perhaps to be a total wreck.

FISHING.

From the days of the aboriginal inhabitants of Block Island, its surrounding waters have been pre-eminent as fishing grounds.

Sea food was a favorite with the American Indians generally, and with the Manissees formed an important share of their food supply, as it also does to the present inhabitants of the island.

There seems to be current an erroneous notion that a large majority of the Block Islanders are fishermen, while in fact about two thirds of them are principally engaged in agricultural pursuits, by whom culture has been carried to every hill-top.

Notwithstanding this fact, the fisheries are a very important source of income to the inhabitants, the total revenue amounting annually to about $75,000, and without which the island would scarcely be able to sustain so dense a population.

The cod, mackerel, and swordfish are those chiefly sought for commercial purposes, although, since the enormous influx of summer visitors, the famous Block Island bluefish, so much in demand by them, forms an important addition to the list.

Since the establishment of the National Harbor, forming a safe and convenient anchorage, large numbers of fishing smacks, from various ports all along the New England coast, resort here during the fishing season to vie with the island fishermen, much to the disgust of the latter, whose gains are thereby considerably diminished.

A great variety of craft are engaged in this industry, but the most interesting are the peculiar Block Island boats, which have attracted the attention of nautical men wherever they have wandered.

An inhabitant of the island thus describes them:—
" They are the ablest sea-going *undecked* craft in the world, and there does not once in five years occur a storm so perilous that the largest of these boats, well-trimmed and ably manned, cannot pass to and fro between the island and Newport. They are from twelve to thirty-five feet in length, and the largest of them will carry from ten to fifteen tons, and draw about six feet of water when loaded. They are lap-streaked, and built of very thin cedar, from one half to seven eighths of an inch in thickness. Their knees and timbers are of oak, and very strongly and lightly made. They are primarily and principally sea boats, and are not, as compared with other vessels, remarkable for speed when going with a free wind, or in light weather; but in a deep sea, close hauled, and especially during heavy gales of wind, they are unusually fast. They carry two sails, a foresail and a mainsail, the foresheet leading aft. The origin of their model is unknown." Their distinguishing fea-

THE FISHING FLEET.—THE START AT DAWN.
(By permission from Lippincott's Magazine.)

ture consists in being pointed at both ends, with the stern and stem posts rising at an angle of forty-five degrees from the keel, and also in having two slender masts, without shrouds or jib-stays, and carrying two narrow, tapering sails.

"The fishing grounds are many in number, and designated by a great number of names, 'Covill' being one of the most popular. Most of these are situated on the bank, so-called, it being an irregular ledge of rocks about twelve miles south of Block Island and from ten to fifteen miles in length, with deep water within and beyond it. The proximity to this ledge is determined by sounding, and the particular grounds upon it in clear weather by ranges on the land; but in foggy weather, when the land cannot be seen, some of the old fishermen will steer so accurately, making calculations on wind and tide, and know so well the depth of water on all parts of it, that they will go day after day, and anchor on a particular spot, not more than a quarter of an acre in area, as certainly and surely as though on land. Coggeshall Ledge, a famous fishing-ground for late spring and summer fishing, is about thirty miles southeast from the island.

"The spring codfishing here commences about the first of April, and lasts until about the first of June, though cod, to some extent, are caught through the summer months. An average share per man for the spring fishing would be perhaps twenty quintals, though sometimes they do not get half that, and occasionally hand shares of seventy-five quintals have been divided.

"Block Island codfish are in high demand, owing to the fact that they are dressed within a few hours after being caught, and thoroughly salted and cured. When the fish are brought ashore, they are thrown into five equal heaps, one of which the owner of the boat takes, and its technical appellation is 'standings.' The rest are equally divided amongst the crew, owners and all." Each man then proceeds to dress his own fish, which being completed, they are carried to the fish-house, counted, and placed in pickle preliminary to drying. The honor of "high hook" is then conferred on the fortunate winner of the greatest number.

Through the month of July the waters in the vicinity of Block Island abound with swordfish, the increasing demand for which in late years has caused a large number of craft to engage in their capture. The visitors to the island during this period have therefore a rare opportunity to accompany some of the fishermen and witness the procedure, which is very interesting, and often becomes a most exciting sport.

The favorite fishing grounds are to the southeast of the island, the large boats often making out thirty miles or more.

The fleet usually leave the harbor between four and five o'clock in the morning, not all at once, but as each feels inclined. "First a skipper more active than the others hoists his sail, darts through the rift in the breakwater, and passes swiftly out upon the heaving, tumbling waters; another and another quickly follow, until in a short time the whole fleet, in straggling line, or two or three abreast, is speeding over the waves." During the outward run the fleet keeps well together until they near the haunts of the swordfish, when one of the crew mounts to the foretop and keeps a sharp lookout. Having descried one of these extraordinary "ocean swordsmen" sporting in the distance, he directs the course of the boat, and the chase begins. Active preparations are commenced on board, and "one of the crew runs nimbly out upon the bowsprit and leaning against the semicircular iron band that tips the stanchion, unlashes the long harpoon, which, from the radiating character of the many iron prongs, is called the lily-iron. The rest of the hands see that the rope attached to the pole is not fouled with the downhaul, that the coil in the tub is in shape, and that the gayly painted keg at the end of the rope is ready for use. By the time these minor details have been attended to, the sharp dorsal fin of the huge fish may be seen from the deck, cutting the sea and rushing about in an erratic manner." Soon the boat is skilfully brought down upon him, when, with marvellous dexterity and unerring aim, the lily-iron is cast, the rope quickly paid out, and the keg thrown overboard. Then ensues an exciting chase after the keg, which acts as a buoy to mark the course of the swordfish in his death-struggle.

After he has become exhausted, the keg is picked

THROWING THE LILY-IRON.
(By permission from Lippincott's Magazine).

up, and the line hauled in until the monster appears on the surface, when with strong lines and pikes he is soon on the deck.

The average size of the swordfish caught about the island is about two hundred and fifty pounds, but frequently the boats bring in fish double that weight.

It is of a long and roun led body, largest near the head, and tapering gradually to the tail, which is remarkably forked; its skin is considerably rough, its back black, and belly of a silvery white. It is most remarkable for the shape of its snout, which is extended in the form of a sword in the upper jaw, the under being much shorter, and terminates in a very sharp point.

A curious fact in regard to them is that they breed on the other side of the Atlantic, and hence young ones are rarely found here.

The capture of swordfish is one of the most ancient pursuits on record, they being held in high esteem by the ancient Greeks and Egyptians, whose method of taking them was identical with ours. They are very pugnacious, and many instances might be cited of attacks made on ships. In 1871, the yacht " Red Hot," of New Bedford, used by Professor Baird of the fish commissioners, was sent to the bottom by one. Specimens of ship-timbers pierced by swordfish may be seen at the Boston Natural History Rooms, also in Philadelphia Academy of Natural Sciences.

The swordfish industry has become a very important one here, and tons of them are annually shipped to New York and Boston.

Another valuable fish taken is the mackerel, and when they are in the offing in June, the Block Island fleet, joined to the stranger fishermen, sometimes presents a most charming picture. "As they anchor at night," to use the language of another, "under the lee of the island, the lights in the rigging, the fantastic forms of the men dressing the fish, the shouts of old shipmates recognizing each other, the splash of the waves, the creaking of the tackle, the whistling of the wind, the fleecy clouds flying across the face of the moon, conspire to make a picture that seems more like a fairy vision than a reality."

The famous Block Island bluefish are taken all through the hotel season. They are generally larger than those caught at points along the adjacent shores of the mainland, and are very abundant. The method of catching them by trolling from a small sailboat combines an exhilarating little cruise about the island with the genuine sport of landing the gamey fish, and has deservedly become a favorite recreation with the summer visitors.

Tautog are also very abundant about the island, and although generally held in high esteem elsewhere, very little attention has been given to them here, thus far. An increasing interest, however, seems to be showing itself in regard to this excellent table fish, and the few who have engaged in their capture have been well repaid The lobster-fishing about the island forms quite an important industry, and is of especial interest to the patrons of the

THE LAST STRUGGLE.
By permission from Lippincott's Magazine.

hotels, inasmuch as they are assured of an abundance of them fresh from the sea.

In 1867 a company of islanders introduced here the device known as a "pound," and the success of this method of catching fish proved so great that a number of them are now maintained, all on the west side.

"A pound is the marine counterpart of a corral," and consists of a long row of spiles driven into the sea bottom, and extending usually about a quarter of a mile directly off shore, against the sides of which cotton netting is fastened, forming a sort of submarine fence, which is called the "leader," and which terminates in a heart-shaped structure constructed in a similar manner. The small end of the "heart" has an opening which leads into an enclosure, made also of spiles and netting, and some fifty feet square, with a bottom of netting, and which constitutes the "pound" proper.

The operation of the pound is very simple. Cod, scup, mackerel, bluefish, foraging along the coast, and approaching from either side, are stopped by the fence, and proceed to swim around by the deep-water end, since they cannot pass on the shore side; at the end of the leader they enter the heart, and still seeking deep water, enter the pound through the aperture, from whose intricacies they rarely escape. Every morning the pound-keepers row out and lift one side of the pound, thus throwing its inmates in a heap on the other, whence they are taken out with wire baskets.

The inland waters of the island also abound in fish, particularly the Great Pond, which affords a source of much pleasure to many who are unable to withstand the ocean swell, while the pond is yet large enough to afford a delightful sail. Frequently large parties of ladies and gentlemen, equipped with well-filled lunch-baskets, make excursions to the Great Pond, which is becoming more popular every season as a place of recreation.

To those well initiated in the fisherman's art, the black bass found in the Bass Pond exercise a fascinating influence, and some of the more skilful anglers have captured some particularly fine specimens.

To the expert, Block Island offers one of the finest opportunities on the coast for striped bass fishing, and there is no doubt that this sport outranks any angling in the world. The southern coast of the island has become famous among adepts in this art, for the great size and abundance of these gamey fish, and fishing-stands have been erected all along the shore, where the devotees of this most refined of all sports may always be found when the sea is in a favorable condition. The largest striped bass ever caught here is reputed to have weighed one hundred and six pounds. Last season numbers were caught that ranged between forty and fifty pounds.

When we take into account the necessity for a kind of recreation which shall not be too violent for the thousands of debilitated citizens who are pent up in squares of brick and mortar, and engaged in sedentary occupations, it is impossible to estimate the value of fishing, as combining so many important features. "It is sufficiently free, airy, and attractive to inflate the lungs, jog the biliary organs, and unbend the mind, and is not so difficult to pursue as to prevent the most delicate physique from enjoying it."

INHABITANTS.

ALTHOUGH generally considered as mere dependencies of the main land, islands almost universally differ from it, not only as to climate and productions, but also as to the individuality of their inhabitants.

A truthful delineation of the peculiarities that characterize any individual or community is a difficult and delicate undertaking. To attempt such a portrayal of the inhabitants of Block Island appears of such insuperable difficulty that only the salient features will be alluded to. The historian informs us that "the Block Islanders are almost wholly descendants from genuine primitive New Englanders."

No other settlement in this country has remained so unmixed and free from foreign elements. They are a very clannish people, and have married and intermarried until practically amalgamated into one great family, with some of the attendant evils. As a physiological study as to questions of consanguinity, they afford a rare field for observation.

There are certain conditions of hereditary organic quality, difficult to describe yet easily perceived, which "render the oak, oaken ; the tiger, tigerish ; and man, human," exercising a more potential influence on the individual than any other cause.

In view of this the Block Islanders are also exceedingly interesting, as exponents of that peculiar mental and moral bias of the Puritan first settlers, who, we are told in Macaulay's History, " mistook their own vindictive feelings for emotions of piety, . . . and when they had worked themselves up into hating their enemies, imagined they were hating the enemies of Heaven."

Physically, they are a hardy, healthy people, and as one writer says, " with good living and good climate, industrious habits, freedom from the anxieties of speculation, excessive strife for display, and the fears of want while fish traverse the ocean, they can hardly be otherwise than healthy and of long life."

They are naturally very intelligent, the standard being much in advance of the average rural population on the main land.

A former pastor of the First Baptist Church of Block Island says : " Their frequent visits to the ports along the coast, from Portland to New York, and the longer voyages that some have taken to foreign countries, have given them a good practical knowledge of men and things which makes them persons of better judgment than many who are more extensive readers and more highly refined."

"The women," says a correspondent, "are generally good-looking, with here and there a beauty." Another says : "The women are healthy, with bright eyes and clear complexions, virtuous and true, and as yet without the pale of the blandishments and corruptions of fashion ;" and another, "If lacking in refined education, this is compensated for by a large supply of common sense and native genius."

The emotional element seems to predominate, and they are quite demonstrative. Gesticulations are freely resorted to, and impart a sort of emphasis to their conversation, which is richly interlarded with nautical phrases, the whole assuming the form, in some sections, of a peculiar dialect, the interpretation of which is a matter of no little difficulty. This style of expression has been greatly modified during the past few years, especially in the vicinity of the Landing, owing to the enormous influx of visitors during the summer months, and contact with whom has not been without profit in this respect as well as others.

A large proportion of the inhabitants are engaged in farming, while the remainder are fishermen, excepting, of course, the usual complement of tradesmen and mechanics found in country towns. The "Three Black Graces," Law, Physic, and Divinity, are not even fully represented, there never having been a resident lawyer on the island.

The following statement of the population at

various periods shows the steady growth of the town during two centuries up to 1860, when the highest number was reached, since which date there has been a slight decrease to the present time.

Year.	White.	Indians.	Negroes.
1662 est. . .	30	400	—
1700 approx. .	200	350	—
1800 . . .	714	16	45
1860 . .	1320	1	28
1880 .	1178	1	24

Of the present inhabitants about ninety-seven per cent. are American born, and over ninety per cent. born on the island.

The people are social and hospitable, and almost to a man successful in obtaining a good, plain support from their own exertions. Not a few have accumulated a considerable property, and all have an excellent faculty of keeping what they have gained.

LEGENDS.

From the days of Homer, down through the middle ages replete with those wild tales which were the delight of the peasantry, to the present time, few countries have not been associated with or do not possess some romantic legends. Block Island is no exception, and there are also current among its inhabitants many superstitious notions, doubtless handed down from the early settlers, as they are evidently derived from the English and Scotch folk-lore.

However reluctant the intelligent part of a community may be to own the fact, it must be admitted that superstition in one form or another dwells beneath the surface of most human hearts, although it may frequently display itself in the most disguised or refined form.

Although the writer has collected no inconsiderable amount of material, the scope of his little book does not admit nor call for an extended recital of the same, hence but a few of the more interesting ones will be referred to.

The story of the Phantom Ship has been made famous by Whittier's little poem, the "Palatine," in which it is to be regretted that the inhabitants of the island are unjustly represented as being guilty of the most atrocious conduct.

The popular version of this story seems to be, that early in the last century a ship named the "Palatine" left Holland for America, having on board a large number of passengers who were intending to settle near Philadelphia, and that among the number were many of considerable wealth, having with them money and valuables for the purchase of lands and purposes of trade. This treasure excited the cupidity of the officers of the ship, who contrived a plan to get possession of it. In accordance therewith, the " Palatine" was kept at sea for many weeks, while the passengers were treated with the utmost severity, and their supply of food and water cut off, although there was an abundance on board. By this means the unfortunate Palatinates, to appease their hunger and thirst, were compelled to buy, at the most exorbitant prices, such provisions as these diabolical wretches were disposed to meagerly dole out. "Twenty guilders for a cup of water, and fifty rix-dollars for a ship's biscuit soon reduced the wealth of the most opulent among them, and completely impoverished the poor ones " After a few weeks their number was daily diminished by the death of those who, becoming penniless, succumbed to their terrible fate, and at last, when the fiendish officers, whose villany is "almost unparalleled in the annals of selfishness," were satisfied that nothing more was to be obtained from the few surviving victims, abandoned the ship somewhere in the vicinity of Long Island.

Left without any controlling hand, the vessel floated helplessly about wherever wind and tide might carry her,—"drifting here, drifting there; land always in sight, yet always inaccessible; some dying from weakness and despair, some from surfeit when the crew had gone and the provisions were left unguarded, all more or less delirious, some raving mad."

After drifting, nobody knows how long, she struck on Sandy Point one bright Sunday morning, not far from Christmas Day, and the island wreckers at once made their way out to her, and with the exception of one woman, who persistently refused to leave the ship, removed all the surviving remnant of the passengers (some sixteen in number), and carefully ministered to their wants. All but three of them died, however; but two of the survivors lived for many years on the island, from whom the story of their hardships was obtained.

At flood-tide the vessel floated clear, and an easterly wind springing up, it soon became obvious that she would drive out to sea despite the efforts of the wreckers, whereupon one of their number set the ship on fire for the purpose of compelling the remaining woman to leave the wreck, but she obstinately maintained her place beside her valuables, while the Palatine "drifted away into the gloom and darkness of the stormy night."

"Let us linger for a moment in imagination on the

shore as the ship recedes from sight, and picture to ourselves the wierd, ghastly, and horrible scene,—the beach illuminated by the light of the burning vessel and dotted here and there by the figures of the wreckers and boatmen, the fierce and angry gusts of wind carrying with them blinding whirls of sand, the low, sullen roar of the surf with its blinding spray driven backward into the darkness, the sullen, merciless billows surging to and fro, around and about the doomed ship, all united to form a gloomy, desolate framework to the agonizing picture of that one lone figure for whose life two great antagonistic forces of nature were angrily contending."

> "But the year went round, and when once more
> Around their foam-white curves of shore
> They heard the line storm rave and roar,
>
> "Behold again, with shimmer and shine,
> Over the rocks and seething brine,
> The flaming wreck of the Palatine."

This mysterious apparition is the strangest part of the tale, for no doubt exists that a singular, luminous body did appear off the western shore of the island, when the year came round, and continued to hover about for a century afterwards, being witnessed by scores of respectable people, many of whom were skeptical until they had been eye-witnesses of this extraordinary phenomenon.

Says a writer in *Lippincott's Magazine:* "The hardy fishermen soon discovered that her appearance heralded storm and disaster, nor were they slow in connecting her with the 'Palatine,' which had drifted away from their shores the year before, and which they believed was now being purified by purgatorial fires, her cruel officers doomed to man her fiery decks and haunt the scene of their crimes until this should be accomplished. The apparition caused great excitement among the simple fishermen, and throngs of the curious came to see and judge for themselves of this strange appearance. For a hundred years the light continued to linger about the island, and then suddenly disappeared, and it was believed that the unquiet spirits were finally at rest."

After a lapse of fifty years, the phantom suddenly reappeared in the summer of 1880, an account of which, witnessed by Mr. Joseph P. Hazard, of Narragansett Pier, R. I., was published in the local newspaper at that time, as follows :—

"When I first saw the light, it was two miles off the coast. I suspected nothing but ordinary sails, however, until I noticed that the light, upon reappearing, was apparently stationary for a few moments, when it suddenly started towards the coast, and, immediately expanding, became much less bright, assuming somewhat the form of a long, narrow jib, sometimes two of them, as if each was on a different mast. I saw neither spar nor hull, but noticed that the speed was very great, certainly not less than fifteen knots, and they surged and pitched as though madly rushing upon raging billows."

Much interest having been expressed by the public

THE PHANTOM SHIP.
(By permission from Lippincott's Magazine.)

in the phenomenon since this announcement, and many speculations advanced, perhaps the following account by Dr. Aaron C. Willey, a well-known physician, who was a resident of the island for a number of years early in the present century, may be read with interest.

BLOCK ISLAND, Dec. 10, 1811.

DEAR SIR: — In a former letter I promised to give you an account of the singular light which is sometimes seen from this place. I now hasten to fulfil my engagement. I should long since have communicated the fact to the literary world, but was unwilling to depend wholly upon the information of others, when by a little delay there was a probability of my receiving ocular demonstration. I have not, however, been so fortunate in this respect as I could wish, having had only two opportunities of viewing the phenomenon. . . . This curious irradiation rises from the ocean near the northern point of the island. Its appearance is nothing different from a blaze of fire; whether it actually touches the water, or merely hovers over it, is uncertain, for I am informed that no person has been near enough to decide accurately. It beams with various magnitudes, and appears to bear no more analogy to the *ignis fatuus* than it does to the aurora borealis. Sometimes it is small, resembling the light through a distant window; at others, expanding to the height of a ship with all her canvas spread. When large, it displays either a pyramidical form, or three constant streams. In the latter case, the streams are somewhat blended together at the bottom, but separate and distinct at the top, while the middle one rises rather higher than the other two. It may have the same appearance when small, but owing to distance and surrounding vapors, cannot be clearly perceived. This light often seems to be in a constant state of mutation; decreasing by degrees it becomes invisible, or resembles a lucid point, then shining anew, sometimes with a sudden flare, at others by a gradual increasement to its former size. Often the mutability regards the lustre only, becoming less and less bright until it disappears, or nothing but a pale outline can be discerned of its full size, then resuming its full splendor in the manner before stated. The duration of its greatest and least state of illumination is not commonly more than three minutes: this inconstancy, however, does not appear in every instance.

After the radiance seems to be totally extinct, it does not always return in the same place, but is not infrequently seen shining at some considerable distance from where it disappeared. In this transfer of locality, it seems to have no certain line of direction. When most expanded, this blaze is generally wavering, like the flame of a torch. At one time it appears stationary, at another progressive. It is seen at all seasons of the year, and for the most part in the calm weather which precedes an easterly or southerly storm. It has, however, been noticed during a severe northwestern gale, and when no storm immediately follows. Its continuance is sometimes transient, at others throughout the night, and it has been known to appear several nights in succession.

This blaze actually emits luminous rays. A gentleman, whose house is situated near the sea, informs me that he has known it to illuminate considerably the walls of his room through the windows. This happens only when the light is within half a mile of the shore; for it is often seen blazing at six or seven miles distance, and strangers suppose it to be a vessel on fire.

This lucid meteor has long been known by the name of the Palatine light. By the ignorant and superstitious it is thought to be supernatural. Its appellation originated from that of a ship called the "Palatine," which was designedly cast away at this place, in the beginning of the last century, in order to conceal, as tradition reports, the inhuman treatment and murder of some of its unfortunate passengers.

From this time, it is said, the Palatine light appeared, and there are many who firmly believe it to be a ship on fire, to which their fantastic and distempered imaginations figure masts, ropes, and flowing sails.

The cause of this roving brightness is a curious subject for philosophical investigation. Some, perhaps, will suppose it will depend on a peculiar modification of electricity, others upon the inflammation of hydrogenous gas. But there are, possibly, many other means, unknown to us, by which light may be evolved from those materials with which it is latently associated, by the power of mechanical affinities.

I have stated to you facts, but feel a reluctance to hazard

any speculations. These I leave to you and to other acute researchers of created things. Your opinion I would be much pleased with.

     I remain yours, etc.,
           AARON C. WILLEY.
HON. S. L. MITCHELL.

 Although Dana in his most brilliant poem, "The Buccaneers," has given poetically accurate descriptions of the island localities, and introduced the feature of a burning ship in a very effective manner, it is entirely the work of imagination, and no such character as Matthew Lee ever

   "Held in this isle unquestioned sway."

 There are many interesting Indian legends associated with the early history of Block Island; however, but one will be presented,—that of Weencombone, a Montaug of great prowess, taken from the collection published by J. A. Ayres, of Hartford, Conn.

  "Whose step is like the prancing deer,
  When quick alarms sound in his ear,
  Or like the swift fox gliding by,
  Gone ere his form you can espy?
       Weencombone.

  "Whose heart is brave when dangers come,
  Or war affrights our tranquil home;
  Who leads the fiery conflict on,
  When the war-scalp is lost or won?
       Weencombone.

  "Whose strength is like the pines that grow
  Above Shagwannock's lofty brow?
  Whose eye is like the lightning's gleam,
  Whose voice is like the eagle's scream?
       Weencombone.

" In pride of heart the warrior stood,
In pride of strength, and pride of blood,
Before old men in council met,
The gathered wisdom of the state,
With flashing eye he told his tale,
Whose tidings woke the funeral wail,
When the red sun with glaring light
Dispelled the shadows of the night.

"' But yester e'en the sun went down
Upon Manisses' walls of stone,
When I, with three brave followers, came,
To watch the evening's dying flame,
With patient care we spent the day,
Beneath the crag whereon we lay,
Watching an eagle's eyry there,
Till the bold king returned from far,
With gallant flight, I saw him come,
Unfearing, to his rocky home:
Upon the crag his wing he furled,
Proud as the monarch of the world,
Shook his strong quills, and with a scream
That woke his brooding mate's wild dream,
Looked down upon the rolling sea,
Free as its rolling waves was he.
This arrow pierced the regal bird,
Ere the far cliffs his death-cry heard,
Downward he fell from crag to rock,
And struck the sand with thundering shock.
His heart was rent in twain,
Checked was the blood in every vein,
And every nerve so strong, but now,
Was palsied by the fatal blow.
He could not move his head that lay
Upon the sands of ocean gray,
Or stir his wing, or with strong grasp
My fingers in his talons clasp:
Yet round and round his flashing eye
Turned boldly on his enemy,
With its full power of lofty hate,
On me who fain would be his mate.

"'I plucked the war-plumes, one by one,
That grew above his heart of stone,
And to my scalp-lock bound them on,
Then climbed the cliffs, and idly lay
To watch the fading light of day.
"'Seek we our home, I said at last,
The labors of the day are past,
And gathering vapors in the west
Tell of the coming sea's unrest.
Scarce had I spoke the signal word,
Or scarce my trusty followers heard,
When the wild war-cry of the north
Close at my side burst fiercely forth.
From bush and rock came swiftly on,
Led by Janemo's haughty son,
Five foemen from the mainland sent
Upon our path with foul intent.
Their war-locks on the evening streamed,
Their battle-axes brightly gleamed,
Flashing while round their heads they swung,
And loud the stirring war-whoops rung.
My knife the leader's scalp-lock found,
Beside my belt the prize I bound:
Then turned again to seek the foe,
Turned but to see the fatal blow
That sent Merodinock's brave ghost
To the fair forests of the blest.
I brained the murderer at a stroke
While fierce revenge within me woke,
And sprang my followers aid to yield;
To late, alas! their lives to shield.
Like true men fought the foe and died,
My warriors falling by their side.
And when the last death-shriek arose,
I was alone of friends or foes.'

. . . .

"Old men with reverence heard his word,
His haughty speech their bosom stirred,
And with respect, showed not in vain,
None answered to his tale again.
Forth from the council lodge he passed,
And sought his quiet home at last."

MISCELLANEOUS.

Owing to the brief time available for the preparation of this sketch of the island and its attractions, the original plan has been somewhat modified, and many little details incorporated in the first manuscript have been necessarily omitted from this.

Among the more important subjects which the writer had purposed to consider are the climatic and other conditions existing at Block Island, with reference more particularly to its claims as a health resort.

The fact has been thoroughly established that pure sea air is the most fraught with tonic qualities of any. It therefore seems but just to assume, other things being equal, that sea islands possess natural advantages over the continents, and that the smaller the island, and the more isolated its position, the nearer the approach to the conditions found on the deck of a ship, which is undoubtedly the best place to obtain it. Unfortunately the latter means is in many cases impracticable, and often impossible, owing to the proneness to seasickness.

A little sea island, therefore, seems the only available means, in a large number of cases, for the unfortunate invalid to reap the benefits of this curative sea air.

No island along our coast is so favorably situated as Block Island in this respect, for in addition to the invigorating qualities of its atmosphere, which never partakes of the mixed character of that at the coast resorts, it possesses the most distinct maritime climate of any point on the eastern border of our continent (see article on "Climate" in Appleton's Encyclopædia), and it is well established that the extremes of temperature are much less violent than in the same latitudes on the mainland, owing to the controlling influences of the surrounding water surfaces.

In an excellent article in the *New York Medical Record*, by Holbrook Curtis, M. D., he says of this place: — "The evenings are invariably cool, and one readily gets the impression, walking on the broad piazza of the great hotel, that he is on the deck of an ocean steamer, breathing the purest air, untainted by the dust, pollen, and organic elements which always appear as constituents of the atmosphere on the mainland. During a two months' stay at the island last summer, I had an opportunity of studying the effect of the air on several cases of malarial fever, which had been sent there, and also of observing the very great advantages several phthisical patients derived in being relieved of night sweats. The air is wonderful in its exhilarating properties, and the temptation is strong to laud what seemed to be marvellous results in cases of nervous prostration and insomnia, which had derived no benefit elsewhere."

The sojourner here finds, in addition, an abundance to occupy his attention and keep his mind from fatigue. The social advantages are of the best, and amusements are not wanting outside the hotels.

The island is particularly fortunate in possessing one of the finest beaches on the coast, giving superior bathing facilities, and affording a splendid drive. As the mean rise and fall of the tide here is but three and fifty-nine hundredths feet, a narrower strip is exposed at low tide than at the coast resorts, but as a compensation no unsightly flats are exposed. The carriage drives about the island are numerous, the roads fairly good, and running in an erratic, zigzag manner over the entire island.

Near the Landing is a commodious Roller Skating Rink, and several bowling alleys and billiard rooms.

The facilities for boating are very good, and in addition to the numerous cat-rigged boats and schooners, a small steam yacht is available for pleasure trips.

Close by the Landing is a restaurant having a capacity for several hundred people, where "shore dinners" have been served to the satisfaction of thousands, who visit the island for a few hours, and do not care to dine at the hotels.

The visitor, among other points of interest, must not omit a visit to the cemetery, which is reached by way of the Centre, passing north about half a mile. Here will be found many quaint inscriptions. The oldest inscribed stone the writer has seen is of thick sandstone, without ornamentation, placed upright, and

GATHERING SEA WEED.
(By permission from Lippincott's Magazine.)

bearing date April 5, 1687. "Most of the older stones are of slate, ornamented with the conventional winged skull and scroll borders, precisely like those in the seaboard towns of the mainland," hence it is supposed they, in common with the others, were imported from England already ornamented, and lettered in this country.

The peat supply will also interest many, although comparatively small quantities are now prepared for fuel, coal being generally used.

An important resource of the island is the sea-weed gathered on the shores, many thousand cartloads of which are annually utilized for fertilizing purposes.

Large quantities of the carrageen, or Irish moss, is annually gathered on the west side, and is the source of a considerable income to the islanders.

No wild animals are found on the island, neither are snakes, but immense numbers of wild fowl, such as geese, ducks, and others, make this a stopping place while migrating.

Outline of History.

The Indian name of Block Island was Manisses, or "Island of the Little God," and it was subject to the Narragansetts.

From its prominent situation out in the Atlantic Ocean, twenty-five miles from Newport and a dozen miles from Point Judith on the Rhode Island coast, it was undoubtedly seen by the earliest European navigators who explored the shores of the New World.

It may not be inappropriate to suggest that those hardy vikings of old, whom Professor Rafn not many years since announced had cruised along our coast, traded with the Indians, and one party remained nearly three years in the vicinity of Narragansett Bay, several hundred years before Columbus was born, may, not unlikely, have been the first civilized men to observe this isolated little speck of land.

American historians seem to have taken very little notice of Professor Rafn's statements, some treating them with scorn, others attributing them to Northman pride, and all undoubtedly profoundly ignorant of the Scandinavian language and unwilling to be told anything about their own country from such a source.

Had they, however, given the simple narrative presented a careful examination and been capable of as wise discrimination as has been manifested by the writer of an article first published in the *Providence Journal* in 1869, and since widely known, a very different conclusion would have been reached as to the credibility of these statements of the celebrated Danish archæologist, which have since been confirmed in many important points by recent antiquarian researches.

The earliest account of the island we find is in a letter, the authenticity of which has been doubted, professing to have been written in 1524, by Giovanni da Verazzano, a Florentine, who was dispatched in that year by Francis I., of France, in command of the frigate "Dauphin," on a voyage of discovery.

This letter mentioned it "in form of a triangle, distant from the main land three leagues, about the bignesse of the island of Rhodes ; it was full of hills covered with trees and well peopled, for we saw fires all along the coast. We gave it the name of Claudia of your majesties mother."

One writer thinks the island must have been seen by Estevan Gomez, in 1526; but as it is uncertain whether he was ever in its vicinity, and is positively known to have died the year previous, this suggestion seems worthy of very little consideration.

Nothing authentic appears for nearly a century after the Italian navigator passed its shores, when in 1614, a Dutch trader, Adrian Blok, who had been de-tained at Manhattan Island by the burning of his vessel, built a rude yacht, undoubtedly the first decked vessel made on these shores, and "sailed eastward through the Sound, and discovered several islands, the last of which he called after his own name."

He is the first European known to have explored the island, and mentions finding upon it a numerous tribe of Indians, who received himself and crew very kindly and "regaled them on hominy, succotash, clams, fish, and game."

Soon after this it was put down on the Dutch maps as "Adrian's Eyland," by which name it was generally designated for many years after, and must have been familiar to the Dutch, who were carrying on a prosperous trade with the Indians in its vicinity.

A few years after Adrian Blok's visit, an incident occurred at Plymouth which resulted indirectly in materially affecting the destiny of this little sea-girt isle. John Oldham, a contentious, turbulent man, having been banished from the colony, after a short time returned and tried to breed a revolt, defying the authorities, who soon had him placed where his wrath had time to cool. He was then compelled to pass through a double file of musketeers, every one of whom "was ordered to give him a thump on ye brich with ye butt end of his musket." After this ceremony they ordered him to leave the colony, and we find him soon after engaged in trading with the Indians, making expeditions from Boston overland as far as the Pequot River, known at present as the

Thames River, in Connecticut. In 1636, he fitted out a small sailing vessel, and proceeded from Boston along the coast to the Pequot country. Returning soon after, he called at Block Island for the purpose of trading with the Manisses. According to a writer in the Historical Collections of Massachusetts: — " A certain seaman named John Gallop, master of the small navigation standing along to the Mathethusis Bay, and seeing a boat under sail close aboard the island, and perceiving the sails to be unskilfully managed, bred in him a jealousy whether that island Indians had not bloodily taken the life of our own countrymen, and made themselves master of their goods. Suspecting this, he bore up to them, and approaching near them, was confirmed his jealousy was just. Seeing Indians in the boat, and knowing her to be the vessel of Master Oldham, and not seeing him there, gave fire upon them and slew some ; others leaped overboard, besides two of the number which he preserved alive and brought to the Bay." Oldham's body, not yet cold, was found on board, horribly mangled.

It was supposed at the time that his murderers were the inhabitants of Block Island, but it has since been stoutly asserted that it was previously planned by a number of sachems, who had preceded him from the mainland for the purpose of avenging some great wrong he had committed. As no cause has been assigned for the Manisses committing the deed, and as Oldham was in high favor with the Narragansetts, to whom they were tributary, this solution is not improbable.

Massachusetts was greatly incensed at Oldham's murder, as he had become quite wealthy, and prominent as a politician, and was an energetic man, well suited to advance the interests of the early settlers, who, we are told, preached " peace and good-will " to men, and acquired the reputation of being a motley group of rapacious adventurers.

The quaint old chronicler says : — " God stirred up the hearts of the honored governor, Master Harry Vane, and the rest of the worthy magistrates, to send forth one hundred well appointed soldiers under the conduct of Captain John Endicott." Three other captains, besides other inferior officers, accompanied the expedition, which was commissioned " to put the men of Block Island to the sword, but to spare the women and children."

When they arrived, the Indians made very little resistance, soon fleeing to the woods, where they successfully concealed themselves. The English found two plantations, some sixty wigwams, and about two hundred acres of corn, partially harvested. They destroyed all, stove the canoes, and re-embarked.

From this time Massachusetts claimed the island, and the Narragansetts acknowledged conquest by paying tribute to the governor ; and a letter of Roger Williams indicates that in Rhode Island they were considered " wholly said governor's subjects."

Very little is known concerning it from that time

until 1658, when the General Court of Massachusetts granted to Governor Endicott, Richard Bellingham, Daniel Dennison, and William Hawthorne all its interest in and to Block Island.

Two years later, three of these sold their interest therein to John Alcock, a physician of Roxbury, Massachusetts, who paid three hundred pounds for the three fourths, and immediately started a scheme for its settlement. Having found nine men who agreed to purchase proportionately, they had a consultation together at the house of Dr. Alcock, August 7, 1660, and having determined the plan of procedure, set about building a bark, which was completed early the following year, and sailed from Braintree, Mass., in April, 1661, with their cattle and household effects. The passengers embarked in a shallop at Taunton, being about thirty in number, several other families having joined the company during the winter.

The following September the proprietors met at the house of Felix Wharton, in Boston, and appointed a Mr. Noyes, of Sudbury, Mass., as surveyor, to go with Mr. Faxon to Block Island, and by lot divide unto every man his due proportion,— a record of which division still appears in the old town records, together with the original compact, and names of first settlers, among which the name of Rose is the only one represented among the present population.

Its sixteen proprietors had equal shares in the soil,

which, as Massachusetts had relinquished her claim upon the island, became private property, and was entered upon as a proprietary, members of which afterwards bought from the Indians any rights they might have in it; and though still under the Massachusetts jurisdiction, from its isolation, it was essentially a miniature democracy.

In the new charter from Charles II., granted in 1663 to Rhode Island Colony, Block Island was included in the territory named, and its inhabitants petitioned the ensuing year to the General Assembly, for civil protection. In May, 1664, the Assembly appointed James Sands and Thomas Terry, and empowered them to call a meeting of the islanders, who were to call a third man as their assistant in the local government of the island.

In 1672 they petitioned for their incorporation as a town, which was granted November 3, that year, at which time the name of New Shoreham was adopted "as signs of our unity and likeness to many parts of our native country."

By popular consent, this name is now seldom used except in official documents, conveyances, etc., and in fact the post-office bears only the name Block Island.

In speaking of the early history of this place, Arnold, in his "History of Block Island," says:— "A local history of Block Island would present an interesting study. The traditionary history of the aborigines is full of the romance of war, their authentic history in connection with the whites abounds in stirring incidents. The peculiarities of the English settlers and their posterity, their customs, their laws, and domestic institutions, are among the most singular and interesting developments of civilized life, while the martial deeds of a people within and around whose island there has been more hard fighting than on any territory of equal extent perhaps in America, and where the horrors of savage and civilized warfare have alternately prevailed almost without cessation from the earliest traditionary period down to recent date, would altogether furnish materials for a thrilling history that might rival the pages of romance."

Soon after the settlement of the island, the Indians were placed in bondage, and some negro slaves were owned by the landlords, who, being few in number, had comparatively large estates, and lived in a somewhat pretentious manner.

In the colonial days the island was infested with pirates from abroad, and many believe much treasure to have been buried here.

In 1689, after war had been declared between France and England, Block Island suffered more than her share of trouble, being invaded and plundered several times during that year, and 1690, as it was also during the subsequent wars in 1744 and 1754.

This island was in turn ravaged by the British, during the Revolutionary War.

In the war of 1812, it remained neutral. From this time forward, until the establishment of the National Harbor, there is little to record.

One writer says:—"Its normal state for two hundred years was that of complete isolation. Its inhabitants had little intercourse with the mainland. They tilled their farms, followed the cod to the fishing-banks, intermarried, buried their dead, sustained their own churches and schools, and formed a sturdy, self-sustaining little republic, independent of their neighbors, and careless of the great world without."

Routes to Block Island.

FROM BOSTON.

Train leaves Providence depot at 6.35 A. M., connecting at Providence with the steamers of the Continental Line, which connect at Newport with Block Island steamer, "Geo. W. Danielson." Arrive at Island 3.00 P. M.

Train leaves Old Colony depot at 8.30 A. M., connecting at Newport with Block Island steamer, "Geo. W. Danielson."

FROM HARTFORD, MANCHESTER, AND ROCKVILLE, CONN.

Take morning train on N. Y. & N. E. R. R. about 7.00 A. M. (see time tables), connecting at New London with steamer "Block Island" each week day.

FROM PROVIDENCE.

Commencing July 8, steamer "Canonicus" leaves Providence at 9.15 A. M., touching at Newport at 10.45 A. M., on Tuesdays and Saturdays.

Steamers of Continental Line leave Providence DAILY at 9.15 A. M., connecting with steamer "Geo. W. Danielson" at Newport, for Block Island.

FROM NEWPORT.

The steamer "Geo. W. Danielson" will leave Newport for Block Island at 12.30 P. M., daily (Sundays excepted), connecting with boat from Providence.

FROM NEW YORK.—NEWPORT LINE.

Commencing on or about June 23, the steamers "Old Colony" and "Newport" will leave Pier 28, N. R., foot of Murray Street, at 6 P. M., daily (Sundays excepted) for Newport, connecting with the "Geo. W. Danielson" for Block Island; returning, leave Newport at 9 P. M. Sundays, take Fall River Line for Newport. Tickets sold and baggage checked through.

NORWICH LINE.

The steamer "City of Worcester," leaves Pier 40, N. R., foot of Watts Street, next pier to Desbrosses Street, Penn. R. R. Ferry, New York, at 5 P. M. Tuesdays and Thursdays. Steamer "City of Boston," Mondays, Wednesdays, and Fridays. Each boat, on alternate days, from New London, connecting each way with steamer "Block Island" for Block Island.

FROM NORWICH, NEW LONDON, AND WATCH HILL.

The new and elegant steamer "Block Island" leaves Norwich at 8 A. M. daily on and after July 1 (Sundays excepted); New London at 9.30; touches at Watch Hill; arrives at Island at 12.30 P. M.

INDEX.

Adrian's Eyland
Adrian House
Advantages of climate
Amusements
Animals
Aqueduct, proposed

Ball, Hon. Nicholas
Baptist Church
Bar, Sandy Point
Bass, black
Bass, striped
Bass Pond
Bathing Beach
Beacon Hill
Bellevue House
Black Rock
Black Sand
Block or Blok, Adrian
Block Islanders
Block Island boats
Block Island House
Block Island Sound
Bluefish
Bluffs
Boats, fishing
Boats, pleasure
Boulders, structure of
Breach, the

Cable
Cemetery
Central Hotel
Centre, the
Chagum Pond
Charter of town
Clay Head

INDEX.

	Page
Cliffs	15-27
Climate	107
Codfish	83
Connecticut House	50
Conquest of Block Island	116
Coonimus	23
Corn Neck	25
Creek, the	31
Crescent Beach	12
Death, first on the island	33
Dialect of islanders	94
Dickens' Point	23
Discovery	112
Divisions	12
Dorrie's Cove	23
Drug Store	60
Ducks, wild	111
Dunes	26
East Side	12
Expedition against Indians	116
Farmhouses	34, 56
First Church	57
First Public House	42
First Settlers	117
Fisheries	80
Fish-houses	41
Fishing	81-92
Filtration of water	29
Fleet, Block Island	81
Fog signal	65
Form of island	8
Fort Island	32
Fresh Pond	32
Fresh water	27
Fuel	10, 111
Gale of September, 1815	14
Geese, wild	111
Geological structure	8, 10
Good Templars	59
Government of island, early	118
Government Buildings	62
Government Breakwater	41

INDEX.

	Page
Grace's Point	23
Grant of island to four men	117
Great Pond	29, 31, 91
Growth of population	95
Hall, Music	49
Hall, Odd Fellows'	59
Hall, Town	57
Harbor	36
Harbor Neck	29
Harbor Pond	31
Highland House	52
High School	57
Hill, Beacon	34
History	112
Hostilities	119
Hotels, early	42
Hotels, present	43-56
Hummock, the	26
Incorporation	118
Indians, conquest of	116
Indians placed in bondage	119
Indian Head Neck	29
Inhabitants	92
Inlets, former	31
Insomnia cured	108
Invasion by French	119
Irish moss	111
Iron, magnetic	10
Island, Fort	32
Legends	96
Life Saving Stations	25, 67
Lighthouses	62, 63
Lobster fishing	88
Location	8
Mackerel fishing	88
Mails	59
Malaria	108
Manisses, Isle of	112
Manisses, Hotel	48
Marden, Dr. O. S.	47
Masons, Atlantic Lodge of	59
Meeting-house, First	58

iv   *INDEX*.

Middle Pond . . . .
Mill Pond . . . .
Military telegraph . . . .
Mineral Springs . . . .
Mohegan Bluffs . . . .
Montauk Point . . . .
Mortar cart . . . .
Music Hall . . . .

Narragansett House . . . . . .
Neck, the . . . .
Neptune Hotel . . . .
New Shoreham, adoption of name .
North Lighthouse . . . .
Norwich House . . . .

Ocean View Hotel . . . .
Ocean View Cottage . . . . . .
Occupations . . . .
Oldham, John' . . . .
Old Harbor Point . . . .
Old Mill, the . . . .
Old Pier, the . . . .
Outline of history . . . .
Outline of island . . . .

Palatine, legend of the . . . . .
Patrolmen . . . .
Paving stones . . . .
Peat . . . .
Pebbly Beach . . . .
Pequot House . . . .
Perch fishing . . . .
Phantom ship . . . .
Photographs . . . .
Pier, the old . . . .
Pirates . . . .
Pole Harbor . . . .
Ponds . . . .
Population . . . .
Position . . . .
Post-office . . . .
Pound fishing . . . .
Proprietors . . . .
Public buildings . . . .

INDEX.

Religious sentiment
Residence, T. E. Tripler's
Restaurant
Roads
Rose Cottage
Routes to Block Island

Sand Hills
Sand's Pond
Sandy Point
Sachem's Pond
Schools
Sea Food
Sea Side House
Seaweed
Settlement
Shipwrecks
Shifting sands
Shores
Signal Service, U. S.
Siren, the
Skating Rink
Slaves
Soil
South Light
Springs, the
Spring House
Stores
Streams
Striped bass
Superstitions
Surf Cottage
Surfmen
Sword fishing

Tautog
Telegraph office
Tide
Tidal wave
Timber
Town Hall
Treasure, hidden
Trees
Trimm's Pond

Union House . . . .
U. S. Hotel . . . .
U. S. Life Saving Service . . . .
U. S. Signal Service . . . . . .

Water, supply of fresh . . . .
Wars . . . .
Weencombone, legend of . . . .
West Side . . . .
Wood . . . .
Woonsocket House . . . . .
Wreckers . . . .
Wrecking . . . .

www.ingramcontent.com/pod-product-compliance
Lightning Source LLC
Chambersburg PA
CBHW021918180426
43199CB00032B/435